Sociology in India

Sociology in India

A Perspective from Sociology of Knowledge

SECOND EDITION

Surendra Sharma

(With a New Introduction by K.L. Sharma)

RAWAT PUBLICATIONS

Jaipur • New Delhi • Bangalore • Guwahati • Kolkata

ISBN 978-81-316-1023-7 (HB)
ISBN 978-81-316-1024-4 (PB)

Second Edition, 2019

Published by
Prem Rawat for **Rawat Publications**
Satyam Apts, Sector 3, Jawahar Nagar, Jaipur 302 004 (India)
Phone: 0141 265 1748 / 7006 Fax: 0141 265 1748
E-mail: info@rawatbooks.com
Website: www.rawatbooks.com

New Delhi Office
4858/24, Ansari Road, Daryaganj, New Delhi 110 002
Phone: 011 23263290

Also at *Bangalore, Guwahati* and *Kolkata*

Typeset by Rawat Computers, Jaipur
Printed at Nice Printing Press, New Delhi

Contents

Acknowledgements

The present study is the outcome of my research work pursued at the Centre for the Study of Social Systems, Jawaharlal Nehru University, under the supervision of Professor Yogendra Singh. I am extremely grateful to Professor Singh for giving me all possible help and guidance during my stay at Jawaharlal Nehru University. Professor K.L. Sharma of JNU helped me in various ways, first in completing this work and then in making it publishable. I am thankful to him for his acts of kindness.

I wish to sincerely thank my friend, Gurchain Singh, a PhD scholar at JNU, for carrying out corrections in page-proofs meticulously, and also for preparing the index with apt attention and care. His good wishes have always been a source of hope and inspiration for me. I express my thanks to Mrs Santosh Tanwer, a PhD student at JNU, for her help in varied ways in making this project a success. Finally, I express my thanks to Mrs Prem Rawat for publishing the volume in a short span of time.

Surendra Sharma

Introduction

Sociology in India is now a fairly grown up discipline. As a discipline, sociology has analysed social-structural units, namely, caste, family, kinship and village community. Class relations in rural, urban and industrial settings have also been studied. Political sociologists have undertaken studies of elites, leaders, political parties and factions. Thus, substantial sociological writings are available, but no proper formulation of criteria of evaluation of these researches has come forth. The relevant questions have not been asked about the nature of theoretical frameworks and methodological devices. The researchers have not stated explicitly about the relevance of their research activities. Why a particular framework has been preferred over some other ones, remains an unanswered question. Why a particular set of hypotheses and certain methodological strategies also remain unstated. What is the 'fit' between a given theoretical framework and particular research design? What is the nature of a framework accepted for guiding research? Questions regarding the philosophical and ontological foundations of theory and method of study have remained quite vague.

We wish to touch upon these questions on the basis of sociological analyses and researches on Indian society covering the post-independence period. The point is: How sociology has grown as a discipline in India? We have focussed mainly on theoretical and methodological aspects of sociological researches in India. Our intention is not to have a pedigree of sociologists and their contributions but to understand the nature of input of knowledge into frameworks and methods of study and the nature of knowledge and understanding that has been produced.

The question about the nature of Indian sociology, its theories, concepts and methodology has been raised repeatedly not only by its founding fathers, namely, G.S. Ghurye, Radhakamal Mukerjee and D.P. Mukerji, but it has also been highlighted through a debate in *Contributions to Indian Sociology* and *Sociological Bulletin.* Without prejudging the theoretical orientations of the participants in the debate, let us state that Louis Dumont and D.F. Pocock set the tone of the debate in the first Number itself of the *Contributions to Indian Sociology* in 1957. They invited F.G. Bailey to offer comments on their perspective on Indian sociology vis-á-vis Indian society. Bailey's alternative perspective was not accepted by Dumont as stated in a rejoinder to Bailey's comments. Dumont has almost totally rejected the 'village studies' reported in two volumes edited by McKim Marriott and M.N. Srinivas, respectively, in 1955. He does not find much theoretically and substantively in Iravati Karve's, *Kinship Organization in India* and A.K. Saran's traditional theory of society and man. A sort of academic contempt is expressed by Dumont against A.R. Desai's study – *Social Background of Indian Nationalism.* The issues highlighted by Dumont and others on Indian sociology have been taken up prominently in our discussion. However, the debate has not remained confined to the pages of the *Contributions to Indian Sociology* and *Sociological Bulletin.* It has also appeared prominently in *Sociological Bulletin* and other journals. A couple of volumes have also appeared on the debate.

A sociology of knowledge perspective has not been articulated in most of these studies, barring a few articles, hence the present study. The points regarding the 'fit' between theory, method and data in Indian sociology, the nature of ideological influences on the understanding of Indian society, the way to construct social reality in the Indian context and the nature of Indian society vis-á-vis Indian sociology are the key elements of the sociology of knowledge perspective. We have stated these points in Chapter 3, specifically in regard to sociology in India, and in a general way in Chapter 2.

The role of the idealist, the positivist and the Marxist traditions has been discussed in this study.

It would be proper to mention the objectives and method of our study and to give a brief introduction to the study itself. The parameters of sociology of knowledge have been discussed in Chapter 2. Sociology of knowledge analyses the relationship between knowledge and existence (reality). We have stated about the paradigms of sociology of knowledge as suggested by Mannheim, Stark and Merton, but more specifically, we have discussed the phenomenological perspective and the perspectives of Marx, Weber and Durkheim. The main points in these perspectives are their epistemology, philosophy, theory, methodology and field of study. However, in regard to the debate about the nature of Indian sociology, we have discussed mainly theory, method and field of study.

The burden of Chapter 3 is an understanding of the foundations of sociology in India as a social science discipline. Ghurye combined diffusionist perspective with Indological orientation and had catholicity in guiding doctoral research. Radhakamal Mukerjee maintained that both the Western social science model and the Marxist model were inadequate for understanding of Indian social reality. A human general theory of relativity was preferred by Mukerjee which combined the particularistic as well as universalistic criteria. However, A.K. Saran finds sociology in India more as a response to the impact of Westernization. An Indianized version of the Marxist approach with emphasis on the study of dialectics of Indian tradition is found in various writings of D.P. Mukerji.

We can discern different orientations in Indian sociology on the basis of theory, method and field of study, followed by various sociologists. Iravati Karve followed a mixed approach, combining Indological, anthropological and diffusionist elements. A combination of Indology and fieldwork (with tilt towards survey research) is found in K.M. Kapadia's studies of marriage and family in India. Y.B. Damle expresses his preference for functionalism of T. Parsons and R.K. Merton, whereas Indra Deva and Yogendra Singh prefer to use general frameworks for studying Indian society and then suggest modifications in them on the basis of India's specific realities. However, A.R. Desai's studies have unequivocally applied the Marxian theory and method for studying Indian society. Lately, Ramkrishna Mukherjee has been engaged in evolving a 'diagnostic' approach with the help of a set of questions with a view to have a proper analysis of Indian social reality and to assess the available sociological studies. We have also discussed the papers presented in two seminars in the 1950s, and the 1960s, one at Agra and the other at Mount Abu.

In a forthright way Bela Dutt Gupta exposes some of the misconceptions about sociology in India. She argues that the local history and the indigenous development of sociology in India and more specifically in West Bengal have not been properly studied. Social and religious prejudices did not stand in the way of accepting natural science models and methods. However, colonialism certainly had an effect on intellectual and scientific development in India. Sociology in India began around the middle of the 19th century. It had a secular basis, and it had its origin in the specific problems of Indian people. It is wrong to say that it is a late arrival from the Western countries. In fact, Gupta says that it is almost contemporaneous to sociology in the West, and it has its independent footings. Gupta makes these observations on the basis of her study of the development of sociology in West Bengal, in particular.

The way the debate on the nature of sociology in India has emerged has been analysed in Chapter 4. The discussion centres around whether sociology in India refers to the study of values or to the study of social relations? Whether the approach should be Indological (or culturological) or comparative? Another question is: Whether sociology should have a 'home-made model' or an 'external point of view' or a mixture of both? The ramifications and variants of these questions have been brought together and discussed in detail. The essence of all these cognitive explorations is only one straight question: What is the nature of sociology in India? We have not found a straight and simple answer to this apparently straight question. There is no chronological order in the shaping of the debate. The same questions have been put back and forth over a period of twenty-five years from 1957 to 1982, which we have covered in our study. However, our main concern, namely, a review of the debate from the point of theory, method and data, does not become secondary. We have examined Dumont's perspective – 'a sociology of values', and have shown that how it could be treated as a value-loaded sociology. F.G. Bailey's comments have been highlighted in this context as an alternate perspective to Dumont's view. To us, Dumont's advocacy of idealizing and particularizing India's social reality seems to be an effort towards indoctrination of sociological analyses and researches. The idea of unevenness of Indian society is illusive, it ignores the vastness of variations and complexities not only of social relations, but even of values and value-premises.

The debate shows prominence of Dumont's thesis from 1957 to 1966, but it takes a turn from 1966 onwards when Dumont stops publication of the *Contributions to Indian Sociology* (Old Series). It is true that the Marxist perspective does not have its due, both in the pre-1966 and the post-1966 periods of the debate. However, Dumont's view is seriously challenged by other variants of the non-Marxist thinking. J.P.S. Uberoi talks of a close tie between Science and Swaraj (Independence). Y. Singh observes (following R.K. Merton) that theory is rare and approaches are far too many. He considers Dumont's view theoretically simplistic and static. D. Narain feels that Dumont's view does not refer to urgent and contemporary issues of Indian sociology. For him, sociology is different from Indology and history, it is empiric and hence synchronic. We have discussed a variety of dispositions of Marxist nature also in Chapter 4 and particularly from the point of their comparison with the non-Marxist dispositions. Specially, in regard to the use of methods and techniques in Indian sociology, we have made reflections on researcher's consciousness about goals of research and the implications of his/her research itself.

Thus, Chapter 2 provides a theoretical blueprint of the sociology of knowledge perspective, the third outlines the theoretical and philosophical foundations of Indian sociology, and the fourth analyses the basic issues in sociology in India from the point of theory, method and data, over a period of a quarter century, from 1957 to 1982. The last two chapters are oriented towards an explication of the perspective outlined in the earlier chapters with regard to a few selected studies of social stratification and village community. Let us state that social stratification and village community have been widely researched aspects of Indian society and a multiplicity of approaches, methods and techniques of research have been applied to the study of social stratification.

From the perspective of theory, method and data, we have analysed structural and processual dimensions of social stratification. Dumont's and Srinivas' studies of caste system have been found by some scholars as quite irrelevant in the present context. Caste as a unique system of social relations, as a model for studying all other aspects, and as an ideological weapon has been questioned not only by Marxist scholars, but also by a variety of non-Marxist scholars. Thus, Chapter 5 focusses on the studies, inspired by the functional, Marxian, Weberian, structuralist and evolutionary perspectives and orientations. The lack of fit between theory, method and data has been pointed out in many cases, but particularly, it has been noted so in the case of Andre Beteille's study of social stratification. Our analysis shows that a good number of Indian researchers have remained insensitive to the implications of theory and method, and generally they have been swayed by the currents of the western theoretical and methodological orientations. A false notion of scienticism and convenience and popularity of a particular method of study have been the major considerations. Indigenization as an approach and method of study has been suggested as an alternative to the above misconceived practice of research.

The sociology of knowledge perspective is further explicated in Chapter 6 for screening a couple of village studies. The views about India's village community, namely, the orientalist, the administrative and the missionary as discussed by Bernard C. Cohn amply suggest that like the 'official view' of the caste system, the 'official view' of the Indian village was the part of the British colonizers of India. The view that Indian village was a 'republic' has given a way to the notions of isolation, homogeneity, self-sufficiency as the main features of the Indian village. Robert Redfield thought of these characteristics in his well-known study, the 'Little Community'. These notions were taken somewhat enthusiastically by others for studying Indian village community in the 1950s and the 1960s. Hence, theoretical and methodological implications of the studies of

Indian village could be seen from the perspective as proposed by Robert Redfield.

The Indian village has been compared with villages in Mexico, England and Africa. But why? M.N. Srinivas', concept of 'dominant caste' comes from the understanding of 'dominant clans' among the African tribes. Historicity of Indian society and Indian village community in particular becomes a serious casualty in most of the village studies. Dumont, for example, looks at Indian village from the point of his approach to the study of caste system.

We have listed the developments in the studies on the Indian village community over a period of a quarter century. The 1950s witnessed a competition between those who preferred Redfield's approach on the one hand, and Radcliffe-Brown's approach on the other. However, both the camps expressed culturology as their main concern. In the late 1950s and the 1960s, the village community was seen more as a structural entity in terms of relationships between higher and lower castes, between Jajmans and Kamins, and between landowners and landless. A number of studies were conducted also from the Marxian point of view.

In fact, we have discussed structural-functional, structuralist and structural-historical orientations in the various village studies. Whether village can be taken as a unit of study or not has been analysed in view of Redfield's view on the one hand, and Dumont's civilization view of caste, on the other. The 'shift' in the 1960s in the village studies has generally been welcomed as it touches upon specific problems of the Indian village community and also emphasizes on the need for indigenization of theories and methods of study. This 'holistic' studies have been replaced to a large extent by the structural and issue-specific studies. Field studies coupled with survey research, historical data and interdisciplinary focus have become more acceptable today.

Finally, a few mundane points about the present study will not be out of context. The present study is an attempt towards pinpointing of main issues, approaches and methods of study in Indian sociology in general, and in regard to the studies of social stratification and the village community, in particular. The study specifically covers a quarter century in Indian sociology (from 1957 to 1982), but as such it is not based on historical method. Our approach is analytical and documentary rather than historical and empirical.

The present study was undertaken only as a prelude for a comprehensive study to be taken, subsequently. A comprehensive study of the kind we intend to attempt would certainly be historical as well as analytical. We may also suggest that the discipline of sociology be investigated, not only from the perspective of sociology of knowledge but also from the point of its structure, process, historicity and contextuality.

New Introduction

*Revisiting Indian Sociology**

K.L. SHARMA**

Initially, Indian sociology was influenced by colonialism and Indology. After independence, Indian sociology moved towards indigenization on one hand and critical examination of the western theories, concepts and methods of study on the other. Indigenization and use of regional texts, sources and observations weakened the western impact on Indian sociology. The idea of the founding fathers of Indian sociology provided a plural and multidimensional thrust to sociology in India. Debates on Indian sociology became intense after Louis Dumont argued for a 'fit' between Indology and the present-day Indian society (sociology). In response to Dumont's view, Yogendra Singh provides a five-fold classification of approaches, and signifies Indian sociology through a synthesis of empiricism and analytical vision. The main contributions to explain Indian sociology have been made by Ramkrishna Mukherjee and Yogendra Singh. Mukherjee talks of 'modernizers of Indian sociology', and Singh looks for 'social conditioning' of Indian sociology.

The main questions are: Sociology for what? Is sociology in crisis? Why do we not work on 'regional sociology'? Whose

* This is a revised version of the Prof. Bela Dutt Gupta Memorial Oration delivered on March 27, 2017 at the Department of Sociology, University of Calcutta.

** K.L. Sharma is formerly Professor of Sociology at JNU, New Delhi. Currently he is associated with Jaipur National University, Jaipur. E-mail: klsharma@hotmail.com sociology are we practising in India? Is sociology not an emancipator? What about 'competition' as the major thrust today in Indian sociology? What is the knowledge input in doing sociology in India? Bela Dutt Gupta (1972) has raised such questions while advocating a need for 'regional sociology'. Answers to these questions lie in what Ronald Fletcher says that sociology is *one*, not *many*. Indian sociology is *one*. Sociology as such is 'evolutionary' and 'developmental', and in the 21st century, it would be one step ahead of the 1900s, as studies of health, education, political power, globalization, marginalization, human rights and social justice may remain the main foci of sociological study and research.

The question is: How theoretically and methodologically sociology has come up as a scientific discipline? Our main concern is with the inputs of knowledge in the making of sociology in the 20th century, and the aspects that would be added to the existing stock of knowledge in the 21st century. The founding fathers laid down the foundation of sociology in India in the first half of the 20th century. G.S. Ghurye combined diffusionist perspective with Indological orientation. Radhakamal Mukerjee found the western social science model and the Marxist approach inadequate as he thought of a general theory of relativity, combining the particularistic as well as universalistic criteria relevant for understanding of Indian social reality. D.P. Mukerji advocated an Indianized version of Marxist model for the study of Indian tradition. The main questions that emerged were as follows:

1. Whether the study of values was more relevant to compare that of social relations?
2. What would be the approach for studying Indian society?
3. Whether an indigenous approach would be more useful than an external one?

Louis Dumont and D.F. Pocock initiated a debate on Indian sociology through their newly edited journal – *Contributions to Indian Sociology*, in 1957. Dumont advocated 'a sociology of values' in the volumes of the *Contributions to Indian Sociology*, published from 1957 to 1966 (known as *old series*). He also advocated idealizing and particularizing Indian social reality, not found elsewhere, in other parts of the world. The principle of pure and impure was perceived by Dumont as the guiding force in all social relations and activities. In the first number of the *Contributions to Indian Sociology* (1957: 9), Dumont and Pocock expressed their views 'for a sociology of India' as follows:

> In our opinion, the first condition for a sound development of a sociology of India is found in the establishment of the proper relation between it and classical sociology. We wish to show how on one side the construction of an Indian Sociology rests in part upon the existence of Indology and how, on the other hand, far from its results being confined to its own domain, it can hope in its turn to widen and deepen the understanding of India, present and past, to which Indology is devoted.

Dumont and Pocock also observed: 'In principle, a sociology of India lies at the point of confluence of Sociology and Indology' (ibid.: 9). 'India is one' and that 'in unity of India is a sort of common place', as observed by Dumont and Pocock (ibid.: 11). Unity is found in ideas and values, and Indian society could be seen through the ideas and values, which are reflected in the caste system and its main principle of pure and impure. While commenting on Dumont and Pocock's approach, Surendra Sharma (1985: 49–51) calls it 'sociology of values or a value-loaded sociology'. Sharma observes that the value-load is evident in their thesis, as according to them, (a) India is one; (b) Indology is representative of people's behaviour; (c) Unity in ideas and values is *social* in nature; (d) unity and differences cannot coexist; and (e) people's mode of thinking and not their modes of actual relations should be taken as data.

Dumont took forward strongly such a thesis through his book – *Homo Hierarchicus* (1970), which is seen by some admirers as a path-breaking treatise on India's caste system and as an apt application of the structuralist approach to Indian society. According to Dumont, hierarchy is a pervasive principle of Hindu society. Cultural meaning is seen by Dumont in caste, kinship, affinity and consanguinity. Dumont finds hierarchy even in what he refers as 'binary opposition', 'pure and impure', 'encompassing and encompassed'. All these imply social relations, in terms of higher and lower ranks/positions.

Right from the beginning, Dumont disapproved of empirical studies of the Indian village, kinship, nationalism, etc., which were narratives/descriptions based on empirical situation and historical data. However, Indian sociology has been influenced considerably by variants of functionalism, Marxism and structuralism. Both specific and general features of Indian society have been analysed. Attempts have been made to see an interlinking of theory, method and data in Indian sociology. For example, Ramkrishna Mukherjee (1974: 169–192) was engaged in working out a 'diagnostic' approach to have a proper analysis of Indian society.

According to Yogendra Singh (1967: 13–37), Dumont's view is theoretically simplistic and static. Indian sociology was limited in its scope, approaches and procedures, and lacked 'positivism' in the pre-independence period. Three main considerations in the disciplinary growth of Indian sociology are: (a) the changing socio-political contours of the country, (b) the changing intellectual relations with the western academia and (c) the native intellectual traditions. In the first two decades, after independence, quantification and abstracted empiricism, experimentalism and arbitrariness in regard to concepts and definitions increased. The early 1960s could be characterized by functionalism, neofunctionalism, historical–comparative method and logico-philosophical and symbolic methods of analysis (Singh as referred in Surendra Sharma, 1985: 41). But the western 'scientism' could not overtake Indian sociology, completely. Singh signifies such a situation as a synthesis of sociological empiricism and analytical quality of vision (ibid.: 41).

The pre-independence sociology as discussed by Singh was descriptive, evolutionary, analytical, comparative and particularistic, while the post-independence sociology could be characterized by (a) the comparative-historical approach, (b) philosophic-sociological approach, (c) logico-philosophical approach, (d) structural-functional approach, and (e) statistical-positivistic approach (Singh, 1967, op. cit. 20). Approaches and views of the entire sociological fraternity could be encompassed in this five-fold classification. Yogendra Singh, however, comments that Dumont and Pocock's view about Indian sociology is largely structural and functional. It is closer to Levi-Strauss' *structuralism* and Durkheim's *functionalism* rather than Radcliffe-Brown's *functionalism*. In fact, Singh is in agreement with Edward Shils' view on Indian sociology. Shils (1961) talks of 'consensual', 'manipulative' and 'alienative' approaches and researches in Indian sociology. Singh finds 'consensus' in structural-functional approach, 'manipulation' in structural-positivistic sociology, and 'alienation' in the comparative-historical and philosophic-sociological approaches.

F.G. Bailey (1959: 88–101), in his critique of the Dumont-Pocock approach to Indian sociology, comments that their style is 'infectious', perspective is too narrow, and they define 'sociology' out of existence. Dumont and Pocock have designed a 'straitjacket' for Indian sociology. In Bailey's view sociology does not consist of a sociology of values; behaviour is equally important basis for abstractions. Bailey does not stand for a particularistic sociology. In Bailey's view, Dumont and Pocock have presented a 'very odd kind of inverted ethnocentrism'. As such, the problem concerning of Indian sociology is: Whether it implies mainly 'sociology of values' specific to Indian society or it is a part of sociology in general, with emphasis on study of structure and change?

Yogendra Singh (1979: 291–314), in his analysis of Indian Sociology from 1952 to 1977, mentions four periods of its trajectory: (a) 1952 to 1960 (philosophical), (b) 1960 to 1965 (culturological), (c) 1965 to 1970 (structural), and (d) 1970 to 1977 (dialectical-historical). This shows that Indian sociologists use conceptual scheme rather than constructing meta–theories or general theories, though there are some exceptions of those who have been guided by theories of Marx, Weber, Durkheim, Parsons, and also by the ideas of Habermas, Foucoult, Derrida, etc. Singh pleads for a synthesis of structural and cultural dimensions in the making of Indian sociology. In general, there is a good deal of theorizing about Indian sociology, but there is hardly any theorization of one's own ideas and researches.

Ramkrishna Mukherjee (1970: 1159–1170) has taken a methodological view regarding the study of Indian society. Mukherjee considers his perspective 'contemporary' as well as 'diagnostic'. Change and development can be fruitfully studied by asking the questions of What, How and Why, at the empirical level. Dimensions of *place*, *time* and *object* are also equally important in the study of developing societies. Mukherjee suggests use of both Marxian and Weberian concepts of social dynamics. He also talks of indicators in terms of the *null hypotheses* and the alternative hypotheses, in a *well-formulated* research design. In two other articles (1973: 1974), Mukherjee refers to four fundamental questions: (a) Why it is? (b) How is it? (c) Why is it? (d) What will it be? Based on his methodological rigour, Mukherjee (1973) works out three stages of the historical development of Indian sociology. These are:

1. Proto-professional stage of sociology prior to the 20th century.
2. Professional stage of descriptive and explanatory sociology in the first half of the 20th century.
3. Currently needed stage of diagnostic sociology (the second half of the 20th century).

Finally, while examining, the role of 'ideology' and deductive-positivistic orientation, Mukherjee (1974: 169–192) appreciates a dialectical ethos with an inductive-inferential orientation. In a comprehensive analysis of 'Trends in Indian Sociology', Mukherjee (1977), while reiterating his diagnostic perspective, raises the following questions:

1. What is it? (Enumeration of the phenomenon).
2. How is it? (Classification).
3. Why is it? (Causality).
4. What will it be? (Probability).
5. What should it be? (Desirability).

These questions imply *descriptive, explanatory, diagnostic* and *positivistic* explanations.

Mukherjee (1979) undertook a comprehensive review of Indian sociology, citing 712 references, covering the profession from 1920 to 1970. A five-fold classification of sociologists is given by Mukherjee, which includes: (a) pioneers (1920–1940s), (b) modernizers (1950s), (c) insiders (1960s), (d) pace-makers (1970s), and (e) non-conformists (1970s).

Yogendra Singh (1986), like Ramkrishna Mukherjee, has undertaken a comprehensive analysis of Indian sociology, based on nearly 700 writings, explaining its 'social conditioning'. There is a clear shift in Indian sociology from the decades of the 1950s and 1960s and early 1970s. The 1970s and 1980s reflect a five-fold typology: *structuralism*, *ethnosociology*, *structural historicism*, *Marxism* and *dimensional* or *systemic* approaches.

The 'social conditioning' of Indian sociology in the first half of the 20th century was reflected in the images of nationalist ideology on the one hand and in the demands for methodology, logic and systemic pedagogy in sociology as a distinct cognitive concern on the other. In the 1950s and 1960s, 'modernizers' of Indian sociology played a leading role. In the 1970s and 1980s, Indian sociology displayed both continuities and changes in its paradigms, social research concerns and issues of identity (ibid.: 15). The questions of 'relevance' and 'indigenization' of paradigms were debated in the contexts of social policy and the role of sociologists in regard to change and development.

Based on a large array of studies during the 1970s and 1980s, Singh (ibid.: 29–30) observes 'two types of orientations emerging in the cognitive structure of Indian sociology both being related to questions of ideology'. The first is that of self-critical autobiographical reflections, and the second is related to cognitive and epistemological issues of sociology. The ideological questions refer to the paradigm shift, indicating the emphasis on the issues of Dalits, gender studies, weaker sections, poor, etc. Singh is of the view that the social conditioning of Indian sociology is reflected in all the phases of its growth in the form of choice of paradigms, substantive areas of research, definitions of the context of relevance and in the interpretation and construction of social reality (ibid.: 102–103).

The last decade of the 20th century could be characterized by sociological studies of liberalization, privatization and globalization (LPG). Since this process began in 1991–1992, now during the past more than two and half decades, new communication technology, trade and commerce across national boundaries, organized retail markets (mega-marts), new middle class in the private sector have emerged, particularly in urban India. Globalization has as such created a crisis of identity for national, regional, and even local cultures, crafts and indigenous markets. But globalization is also a comprehensive and composite concept and a process of change. It has paved a way for understanding of complex linkages, interdependence and integration among countries and people.

Globalization impinges upon the Indian society in general, and upon some specific sections and segments in particular. Besides harmonization, it also destroys diversities and marginalizes national, regional and local cultures and environments (Sharma, 2007). Globalization is viewed as an offshoot of capitalism and modernity (in terms of new-forms and practices). Against globalization, in India, farmers, women, artisans and poor sections of society have launched movements (Sheth, 2004: 45–58).

The recent studies of social mobility, migration and global diaspora are mainly an offshoot of globalization (Singh, 2004: 205–220). Besides these new processes, cultural interaction through media exposure, leisure activities, tourism, entertainment, cultural products, etc. are being reshaped as a result of globalization. In India, for example, organized retail trade is nearly to the extent of 10 per cent only, but its visibility is quite amazing in terms of new markets, branded goods, neat and clean layouts and spaces, disposable income, consumerism, etc. (Sharma, 2016).

According to Yogendra Singh (2004: 208–211), globalization has generated several ideological nuances in its contemporary and substantive evaluation because of its social, cultural and economic consequences. Singh (ibid.: 210) writes: 'In my view, globalization is a unique process. It is a product of such developments in the field of science and technology which are entirely new to human history'. It has created both new opportunities and challenges at the same time. Singh states that the interdisciplinary perspective can help in understanding the social realities due to the double-edged process such as globalization.

A major challenge that globalization has posed refers to the social inequalities in India. Singh asks: How is globalization going to affect various sections of Indian society? How globalization with a slow pace can meet the challenges posed to this very process by the society? The question of identity is a challenge to the process of globalization. Globalization has induced a new process of 'privatization', which implies new forms of economic and social inequalities.

Market, disposable income and middle class, in their new forms, have created new cleavages and inequalities. Who have access to the new market, and who are deprived of it? 'Market mania' and 'market fobia', as explained by Dreze and Sen (2011), are the consequences of globalization. Market as a desirable phenomenon and market as 'fear', a means of inequalitics and disparities, are referred as 'mania' and 'phobia', respectively. Globalization implies a new form of global 'domination', which filters down to different countries, regions and local people.

Recently, some new areas for investigation by Indian sociologists, as suggested by D.N. Dhanagare (2004: 4–30), refer to policy concerns. What should be the future desired type of society and how the problems of 'social' can be tackled was the concern voiced by I.P. Desai (1979: 28 (1–2), 1–8). Dhanagare expressed that 'green revolution' had caused social inequalities in rural India (1987: 22(2), AN-137–144). Many other scholars voiced their concerns in the 1980s and 1990s regarding social tensions, lacunae in land reforms, social reforms, prevalence of violence, etc. Some sociologists have used history in their studies of classical texts, whereas some others have narrated historical background of social reality (Dhanagare, 2007).

In a recent book, T.N. Madan (2013) brings out the state of sociology at University of Lucknow (from 1921 to 1975). The contributions of Radhakamal Mukerjee (1989–1968), Dhurjati Prasad Mukerji (1894–1961), Dhirendra Nath Majumdar (1903–1960), and Awadh Kishor Saran (1922–2003) have been described by Madan. The range of topics covered is quite vast, including (a) cultural values and economic institutions, caste and social change in India, the theory of social institutions, status, ecological and social, and sociology as science and as philosophy (Radhakamal Mukerjee); (b) caste and class, equality and personality, independent India: the immediate problem, intellectuals in India, and Indian tradition and social change (Dhurjati Prasad Mukerji); (c) tribes in transition, tribe and caste: biological and sociological aspects, the village: a concept, a way of life, and sociology as an instrument of social policy; and (d) sociology in India, Gandhi's theory of society, the two contexts of secularization: Western and Indian, and sociology in crisis (Awadh Kishor Saran).

Of all the four scholars at Lucknow University, Radhakamal Mukerjee was an interdisciplinarian in a true sense. Saran was a student of the other three, but practised a theoretico-philosophic stream, rooted in India's past glory and civilizational uniqueness. D.P. Mukerji applied a modified version of Marxism to the study of Indian tradition, its dialectics and change. D.N. Majumdar practised both physical and social anthropology initially, but in the latter half of his academic journey, he was more tilted towards social and cultural anthropology. A.K. Saran was more for exploration of 'traditional thought' and questioned bitterly the notion of 'modernity'. Being a theist, for Saran the idea of a social science was an anathema (Madan, op. cit. 44). Saran rejected English social evolutionism, French positivism, and Marxism.

At Lucknow University, to begin with, and for nearly three decades, Economics and Sociology constituted the same department. This was also the case of Bombay University. Chairs in sociology in 1917 were also set up in Calcutta, Madras and Mysore along with Bombay.

At Bombay, though Patrick Geddes occupied initially the chair in sociology, G.S. Ghurye was appointed as Reader in 1923, and promoted as Professor in 1934. Ghurye thought of anthropological approach to sociology as the most appropriate. A.R. Desai, though a staunch Marxist himself, diversified the discipline of sociology during his tenure as the Head of the Department, and during his tenure, 50th anniversary of the department was celebrated. Desai himself edited two volumes on Modernization (1969). D. Narain edited later on a volume on Family in honour of K.M. Kapadia, and J.V. Ferriera edited a volume in honour of Patrick Geddes. A couple of years ago, A.R. Momin edited a volume in honour of G.S. Ghurye. Ghurye's contribution lies in supervision of nearly 80 students, and in publication of 40 books and several papers, with a great emphasis on Indian civilization and culture in terms of its vastness, diversity and unity. Among the notable students of Ghurye were K.M. Kapadia, Iravati Karve, M.N. Srinivas, I.P. Desai, A.R. Desai, Y.B. Damle, M.S.A. Rao, G.S. Nepali, etc. Ghurye's legacy lies in his catholicity with regard to research students, strong empirical database, and the rigour of scientific discipline (Dhanagare, 2011: 127–157).

Besides Bombay and Lucknow, sociology gained currency in the 1960s at Pune, Baroda, Delhi (Delhi University and later on at JNU), Jaipur, Chandigarh, etc. The main focus was at the Delhi School of Economics, where Srinivasian Sociology became known in India and outside. After more than a decade, sociology at JNU emerged as a far more liberal discipline, with a semblance of Western and Indian perspectives and concepts, under the leadership of Yogendra Singh. His book – *Modernization of Indian Tradition* (1973) has made a great impact on Indian sociology in particular, and social sciences in general.

Shiv Visvanathan (2011: 290–313) explains that 'a civilization question' is absent in sociological debates in post-independent India. Visvanathan (ibid.: 291–292) writes with a lot of anguish as follows: 'Sociology tried to organize itself professionally as a science. It tried to standardize concepts and quantify methodologies. Srinivas' idea of Sanskritization can help explain this process. Just as a lower caste changes its rituals and consumption to imitate a higher caste to raise its status; sociology attempted to scientize its methods or language to raise its status as an academic discipline'. The perspectives such as orientalism, humanism and reimagination vis-à-vis Indian society have further given a big push to the Western hegemony in Indian social sciences. Edward Shils (1961) also observed that sociology in India was a shadow of the Western sociology. However, social movements and struggles of the wretched of the earth have played a significant role in providing sociology/social anthropology a newness, empirically and conceptually.

The pre-independence sociological categories were substituted in the 1950s and 1970s by the categories of caste, kinship, family, village and religion. Later on, the categories of 'class' and 'power' were added. The Indological approach was humbled by way of holistic-monographic studies with implicit functionalist ethos in the 1950s and 1960s. The Srinivasian cultural sociology/anthropology was challenged by macro-categories, like structure, change, development, modernization, legislation, movements, etc. Further, even these categories were questioned by reincarnation of 'culture' in understanding of the 'social'. The ideas of 'honour', 'dignity', 'identity', 'mobilization', etc. received a lot of significance. Along with these conceptual and cognitive advances, the studies of weaker sections, poor, Dalits, women and marginalized groups surfaced, challenging the persisting studies in the discipline of sociology in India.

Sociology for what? Partha Nath Mukherji, the President of Indian Sociological Society (2006: 172–200) makes this question as the theme of his address. He pleads for redesigning of sociology to answer this question regarding reasons for doing sociology. Mukherji expresses his concern for adequate understanding of India's complex, plural, sociocultural realities, rapid transformation, quality of teaching and research, relevant theoretical, methodological and pedagogical innovations, dissemination of knowledge vis-à-vis plurality of Indian society, etc. For doing relevant sociology, Mukherji suggests *canonization* of sociology as a discipline, following Immanuel Wallerstein, and also recommends *conscientization* for self-realisation vis-à-vis the Indian society and sociology in India. Mukherji (ibid.: 175) writes: 'Sociology in India, particularly after independence, in a larger measure, developed in an environment of tension between the social anthropological heritage of Britain, sociology as canonized in the US, and the Marxist intellectual tradition'. After a critical analysis of three theoretico-empirical influences of Indian sociology, Mukherji pleads for a far more comprehensive sociology for India. He writes: 'Sociology, as I understand it, reaches out to all spheres of societal life in a manner that no other social science does. The reason for its all-pervasiveness lies in the *substance* of sociology, namely, normatively defined *social relationships* – between individuals; between and within social groups and institutions of all kinds and sizes, across space and time, in given cultures. Sociology is coextensive with social life' (ibid.: 192). Mukherji further writes: 'It is my argument that all societies need to indigenize their approaches in sociology and the social sciences – much the same way western social science had done historically and continues to do so' (ibid.: 193).

Michael Buraway (2007: 339–354) observes that marketization is destroying the very grounds upon which sociology grows. Sociology as a discipline is more for upholding civil society, and for keeping distance from state and market. Karl Polanyi

(1944/1957) too talks of three waves of marketization, namely, commodification of labour, money and land, and generating counter-movements at local, national and global levels. Sociology gets reshaped with each wave. In the first case, it is utopian; in the second, it is driven by policy concerns, and in the third, it implies public sociology. Going by Buraway, *public sociology* will pave a way for a policy-oriented, critical and professional sociology. 'Public' needs to be at the centre of sociology. Civil society would comprise of a whole of people, institutions and problems.

To engage with 'public', Hetukar Jha (2005: 396–411) emphasises on the need for 'regional orientation' in sociology. Bela Dutt Gupta (op. cit. 1972) was a pioneer in constructing Indian sociology based on a vast treasure of data from Bengal. Several views have been expressed for 'breaking the western hegemony' (Namrata Gupta, 2007: 426–430); 'challenging western paradigm on social knowledge' (Mohanty, 2007: 435–438); 'overhauling of teaching and research' (Gill, 2007: 430–435). There are also views expressed for keeping sociology open to concepts and theories, irrespective of their western origin.

A well-perceived knowledge perspective would facilitate understanding of classifications, consciousness, solidarity, interpretation, creative labour, etc. Using A.W. Gouldner's idea of 'domain assumptions' and 'background assumptions' (1971), a line can be drawn between 'form' and 'substance'. Emancipation from the rigid, static, sterile, outdated, and non-functional concepts, categories, and constructs is a real challenge to sociology at this juncture in the 21st century. A search for 'dominant causality' has to remain an ongoing concern of today's sociologist.

Since the Indian society has not been evolving in a uniform and unilinear direction, the discipline of sociology cannot undermine such a complex social reality. There has always been a social conditioning of sociology, as there is also conditioning of society in terms of internal structure and culture and by the influences external to it. Today, largely the Indian state is shaping social institutions, social groups and processes of change and mobility. Besides the transformed reality of caste, community, family and individual, and 'capital' and its transformation, using Bourdieu's view (1991: 55–56), 'demand groups', such as the unemployed, poor, students, leaders, priests, pontiffs, peasants, professionals, journeymen, women, Dalits, tribals, etc. have a renewed articulation and mobilization.

The Indian sociology faces the following challenges:

1. Challenge of post-modernism and liberalization, privatization and globalization of the knowledge society.
2. Formation of a new order and its differential impact in terms of sources of knowledge and understanding.
3. 'Competition' as a new ethos, affecting 'cooperation' and 'conflict' as the guiding factor in social relations.
4. Complexity of social reality, demanding understanding with interdisciplinary inputs.

We may have to ask:

Whose sociology are we practising? Are we doing it mainly for the urban rich, rural kulaks, middle classes, and power-seeking groups and individuals?

Sociology in India needs to be grounded in the ramifications of the changing structure and culture of the Indian society. There are new parameters of difference and stratification which necessitate a differential sociology. As a sociologist, one needs to know the nature (dynamics) of the state, and its priorities or concerns. As such, sociology can provide clues for reshaping the state and society. Sociology needs to place itself on a higher plane, qualitatively. Without knowing critically the dynamics of teaching and research, we cannot create a strong platform to stand on. From a critical viewpoint, we can identify the discipline and its relative status, compared with its position in other countries and other disciplines. We would like to repeat the often asked questions:

1. How has sociology grown in India?
2. What is the knowledge input in its evolution?
3. How do we relate the Indian sociology to the Indian society?

These questions remain relevant as since independence sociology has undertaken a long journey, from Indology to empiricism, from functionalism to Marxism, from specific sociologies to specific-selective sections and problems. In this journey, the debates such as westernisms vs indigenization, and empirical vs historical approaches have also surfaced. Indological studies have almost disappeared. So is the case of holistic-monographic studies. There was a time when dimensions of 'class' and 'power' were added to the study of caste, mainly to examine the relevance of the views and perspectives of Risley, Ghurye, Hutton, Srinivas and Dumont (Mukherjee, 1957; Beteille, 1966; Sharma, 1974). Today, even the multidimensional studies of caste, class and power are not heard of. And so is the case of the studies of 'green revolution', 'development', 'family', etc. The studies of 'professions', 'movements' and 'civil society' have receded. Studies of Dalits and women sometimes appear, but not with the vigour and emphasis as much as they had two decades ago. The studies of middle classes, migration, mobility, country-town nexus, globalization (perhaps now deglobalization), political power (empowerment), social inequalities, etc. are in vogue, currently.

Looking at such dynamics and dialectics of Indian sociology, we may ask: Is Indian sociology an emancipator? Emancipation implies demystification of ideas, values and norms, notions relating to caste, community, family, marriage, village, religion, rituals, state, etc. Emancipation also paves a way to new concepts and categories, in place of the persisting outdated concepts as insignificant ones. We need 'sociological imagination', specific to Indian society. A renewed 'reflexive sociology' or demythologization/ demystification needs to be created. Knowledge cannot be independent of existence.

Ronald Fletcher's view (1974: 39–69) about sociology as a discipline is quite appealing and convincing. He says sociology is *one*, not *many*. All theories and concepts have been examined as 'evolutionary' and 'developmental' by Fletcher. It is not a question of a 'western' or 'non-western' viewpoint, more important is to see how Indian sociology could be viewed from such a perspective. The studies of Indian society during the 1950s, 1960s and 1970s receded, and emphasis on the studies of gender, state, civil society, empowerment, ethnicity, etc. surfaced during the 1980s and 1990s. Today, sociological studies on health, education, globalization, marginality, human rights and social justice are more pronounced.

We may infer from the above analysis as follows:

1. A search for the 'social' is a basic prerequisite. For example, how 'relations of production' are social or society is *sui generis* or how in a given situation, a particular *interest* (s) is pursued.
2. Dynamics of Indian society or of its specific aspects need to be understood carefully to understand the present and to project the foreseeable future.
3. Sociology needs to connect 'form' with 'substance', to know the 'dominant causality' in a given society/context.
4. Lastly, a critical review of the morphology of the discipline with regard to teaching and research may be necessary.

Indian Sociological Society (ISS) has been engaged in bringing out its official journal *Sociological Bulletin* (SB) since 1951. During the past few years, the ISS has also published a couple of volumes on particular themes based on the papers already appeared in the SB. Besides this, *Indian Council of Social Science Research (ICSSR)* has published several volumes in the form of Trend Reports. Articles published in *Economic and Political Weekly* have also been brought out in the form of edited volumes on themes, like Village, Caste, Tribe, Movements, etc.

Here, we may mention only the latest, a three-volume set, published by the ICSSR (2014), and edited by Yogendra Singh. In all, there are 21 papers in the three volumes.

Singh has given three broad titles to the three volumes: (a) Emerging Concepts, Structure, and Change (Volume-I), (b) Development and Change (Volume-II), and (c) Identity, Communication, and Culture (Volume-III). Singh comments that papers in the three volumes show a trend from consensual to critical orientation. Shifts in conceptual and theoretical paradigms are evident in the studies and analyses. Change in methodological orientation is also evident in the three volumes. Horizons of concepts like caste, village, change and development have expanded. 'Social conditioning' of Indian sociology is being considered as a significant concern. For example, emphasis is on 'field view' of history, 'deconstruction' of the West as a frame of reference, a critique of the philosophical debates in sociology of knowledge, questioning caste as a system/India as a caste society, new rural linkages and country-town interrelations, contradictions and antinomies in the rise of middle class, counter-ideologies of development and politics, and complex and multi-layered urbanism in India.

The emphasis in the decadal reports in the above volumes is on continuity and change. Singh (ibid.: 16) writes: 'No discipline or cognitive stream of thought embedded as it is in history can disinherit itself from its past'. However, there is 'deconstruction', and there are also innovative departures in the use of theories, concepts and methodologies. A great deal of diversification in research has occurred. For example, caste as a system has almost ceased to exist, but 'caste' as a notion/idea, in a quite changed form, has emerged, and it is associated with almost every possible aspect of social life, economy, polity, and even with science and technology. Caste has become a double-edged phenomenon. It has been 'deconstructed', and it has been reincarnated. This applies to many institutions, including family, kinship, religion, etc.

Singh (ibid.: 16–19) talks of five-fold dimensions of continuity and change: (a) a continued emphasis on the relevance of history and past, (b) a continued presence of the 'West' as a frame of reference in discourses, (c) a consistent acknowledgement of a multidisciplinary approach in regard to theory, method and data, (d) an enormous differentiation in substantive foci or concerns, and (e) recognition of the process of globalization in terms of its impact on new forms of social and cultural formations in the society.

Thus, we are not suggesting altogether a new sociology for India in the 21st century. Questions and interrogations have become quite a norm. *Interrogating Caste* (Gupta, 2000) and also *Mistaken Modernity* (Gupta, 2007) or questioning the very nature of Indian Village (Gupta, 2005) are the examples of modifications in the notions which were prevalent in the first few decades after independence. The Dumontian view of caste (Dumont, 1970) has become quite weak as the idea and practice of pure-impure and untouchability have lost their appeal in public life. Caste is everywhere and it is also nowhere. There are new people/groups in the middle classes in India.

We would like to mention (Sharma, 2013) with regard to social stratification in India that new sociocultural, economic, and political considerations have substituted the earlier notions of caste and class. The very criteria of evaluation and ranking are determined by performance/achievement of individuals. Certainly, family plays an important role in an individual's achievement/non-achievement. One can see a new mode of social relations and interactions. Quality higher education, white collar jobs, high income, social networks, etc. determine social status to a considerable extent. Along with 'caste', the working class (both urban-industrial and rural peasantry), differentiation of peasantry, entrepreneurship, new middle class, income inequality, poverty, education, consumerism, lifestyles, caste and class identity etc. are today the main substantive aspects of social stratification in India.

There is a great deal of pluralism in Indian sociology. Varied orientations and methods have widened the horizons of the discipline of sociology. Variants of functionalism and Marxism, structuralism, symbolic interactionism, critical sociology, phenomenology, ethnomethodology, etc. are taught in our universities and colleges, and some scholars have made efforts to find out their relevance to study the Indian society. However, we have mainly used variants of Marxism, functionalism, and to some extent structuralism. Sometimes, such a multiplicity also leads us towards 'unselective eclecticism or futile competition' [Podgorecki and Maria Lo's (1979: 1–4)]. A change or a paradigm shift in the discipline is a sign of its enrichment as 'multidimensional sociology'. For example, specific sociologies, such as industrial sociology, rural sociology, urban sociology, political sociology, etc. would widen the scope of sociology as a discipline.

Indian sociology is certainly plural and multidimensional as it is evident from the publications and the programmes of study and research. Colonialism certainly had an imprint on Indian sociology. But after independence, indigenization of curricula and research has been evident. The nature, scope and status of Indian sociology characterize its pluralism. Certainly, in the first few decades of the 20th century, one could mainly see the impact of colonialism and of the literati of that period. The studies of agrarian relations, green revolution, social movements, change and development provided a different perspective compared to the earlier studies of caste, kinship, religion and the village. Studies in the 1980s and 1990s were quite different, thematically and substantively. Criticisms of functional, Marxist and structuralist paradigms paved a way for new formulations and for their applications. Indian sociology has been a fast growing and dynamic discipline. The whole range of real life aspects covered under its umbrella speaks of its democratic and egalitarian nature.

Today, caste is more a matter of interpretation and a purposive rationality. At the same time, pathologies of modern polity and economy are partly caused by appropriation of caste. A lot of areas are also free of caste, particularly modern occupations, education and access to healthcare facilities. The question is of divides between the rich and the poor, the rural and the urban, the resourceful and the resourceless, the highly educated and the less educated/uneducated. Structural determinants of dominance would determine status and prestige. In other words, what Ramchandra Guha (2008) says about four categories/entities, namely (a) Rights, (b) Riots, (c) Riches and (d) Rulers, would remain as the main considerations in shaping/reshaping Indian society. Indian sociology would revolve around weak/strong Indian state, structuring of social inequalities, reproduction of elites and middle classes, the urban and rural poor, and change from both below and above. As such, Indian sociology is ONE, and a plethora of studies and researches would remain concerned with India's pluralism.

References

Bailey, F.G., 'For a Sociology of India?', *Contributions to Indian Sociology*, No. III, 1959, pp. 80–101.

Beteille, Andre, *Caste, Class and Power*, Bombay, Oxford University Press, 1966.

Bourdieu, Pierre, *Language and Symbolic Power*, Cambridge, Polity Press, 1991.

Buraway, Michael, 'The Future of Sociology', *Sociological Bulletin*, Vol. 56, No. 3, 2007, pp. 339–354.

Desai, A.R., 'Relevance of the Marxist Approach to the Study of Indian Society', *Sociological Bulletin*, Vol. 30, No. 1, 1981, pp. 1–20.

Desai, I.P., 'The Concept of Desired Type of Society, and the Problems of Social Change', *Sociological Bulletin*, Vol. 28, Nos. 1–2, 1979, pp. 1–8.

Dhanagare, D.N., 'Green revolution and social inequalities in rural India', *Economic and Political Weekly*, Vol. 22, No. 2, 1987, AN 137–144.

——, 'Social Policy Concerns in Indian Sociology', *Sociological Bulletin*, Vol. 53, No. 1, 2004, pp. 4–30.

——, 'Practising Sociology through History', *Economic and Political Weekly*, Vol. 42, Nos. 33 and 34, 2007, pp. 3414–3421 and 3502–3508.

——, 'Legacy and Rigour: The Bombay School of Sociology and its Impact in Universities in Maharashtra', in Sujata Patel (ed.), *Doing Sociology in India: Genealogies, Locations, and Practices*, New Delhi, Oxford University Press, 2011, pp. 127–157.

Dreze, Jean and Amartya Sen, *Indian Development and Participation*, New Delhi, Oxford University Press, 2011.

Dumont, Louis and D.F. Pocock (eds), *Contributions to Indian Sociology*, No. 1, 1957.

Dumont, Louis, 'For a Sociology of India: Village Studies, Kinship', *Contributions to Indian Sociology*, No. 1, 1957, pp. 7–64.

——, *Homo Hierarchicus*, London, Weidenfeld and Nicolson, 1970.

Fletcher, Ronald, 'Evolutionary and Developmental Sociology', in John Rex (ed.), *Approaches to Sociology: An Introduction to Major Trends in British Sociology*, London, Routledge & Kegan Paul, 1974.

Gill, Rajesh, 'Let Sociology be Sociology', *Sociological Bulletin*, Vol. 56, No. 3, 2007, pp. 430–435.

Gouldner, Alvin W., *For Sociology: Renewal and Critique in Sociology Today*, Harmondworth, Middlesex, Penguin Books, 1973.

Guha, Ramchandra, *India After Gandhi*, New Delhi, Pan Books, 2008.

Gupta, Bela Dutt, *Sociology In India*, Calcutta, Centre for Sociological Research, 1972.

Gupta, Dipankar, *Interrogating Caste: Understanding Hierarchy and Difference in Indian Society*, New Delhi, Penguin Books, 2000.

——, 'Wither the Indian Village: Culture and Agriculture in Rural India', *Economic and Political Weekly*, Vol. XL, No. 8, 2005.

——, *Mistaken Modernity: India between Worlds*, New Delhi, Harper-Collins Publishers India, 2007.

Gupta, Namrata, 'Universalizing and Indigenizing Social Knowledge: Breaking the Western Hegemony', *Sociological Bulletin*, Vol. 56, No. 3, 2007, pp. 426–430.

Jha, Hetukar, 'Indian Sociology in Crisis: The Need for Regional Orientation', *Sociological Bulletin*, Vol. 54, No. 3, 2005, pp. 396–411.

Kolenda, Pauline, 'Micro-ideology and Micro-utopia in Khalapur: Changes in the Discourse on Caste Over Thirty Years, *Economic and Political Weekly*, Vol. XXIV, No. 32, 1989.

Madan, T.N. (Ed.), *Sociology at the University of Lucknow: The First Half Century (1921–1975)*, New Delhi, Oxford University Press, 2013.

Mohanty, B.B., 'Challenging Western Paradigm on Social Knowledge', *Sociological Bulletin*, Vol. 56, No. 3, 2007, pp. 435–438.

Mukherji, Partha Nath, 'Sociology for What? Rethinking Sociology in an Era of Transformatory Changes, *Sociological Bulletin*, Vol. 55, No. 2, 2006, pp. 172–200.

Mukherjee, Ramkrishna, *Dynamics of Rural Society*, Berlin, Academic Verlag, 1957.

——, 'Study of Social Change and Social Development in the Developing Societies', *Economic and Political Weekly*, Vol. V, Nos. 29–31, 1970, pp. 1159–1170.

——, 'Indian Sociology: Historical Development and Present Problems', *Sociological Bulletin*, 22(1), 1973, pp. 29–58.

——, 'The Sociologist and the Social Reality', *Sociological Bulletin*, 23(2), 1974, pp. 169–192.

——, 'Trends in Indian Sociology', in *Current Sociology*, 25(2), 1977.

——, *What Will It Be?*, New Delhi, The Macmillan Company of India Ltd., 1979.

——, *Sociology of Indian Sociology*, Bombay, Allied Publications, 1979.

Podgorecki, Adam and Maria Los, *Multidimensional Sociology*, London, Routledge and Kegan Paul, 1979.

Polanyi, Karl, *The Great Transformation: The Political and Economic Origins of Our Time*, Boston, Beacon Press, 1944/1957.

Sharma, K.L., *The Changing Rural Stratification System*, New Delhi, Orient Longman, 1974.

——, *Reconceptualising Caste, Class and Tribe*, Jaipur, Rawat Publications, 2001.

——, 'Caste, Class and Globalization: Continuity and Change', in Kameshwar Choudhary (ed.), *Globalization, Governance Reforms and Development in India*, New Delhi, Sage Publications, 2007, pp. 241–258.

——, *Handbook on Social Stratification in the BRIC Countries: Change and Perspective*, Singapore, World Scientific. It is a volume authored by Li Peilin (China), M.K. Gorshkov (Russia), Celi Scalon (Brazil) and K.L. Sharma (India), 2013.

Sharma, Sanju, *Business Ethics and Corporate Social Responsibility*, Jaipur, Rawat Publications, 2016.

Sharma, Surendra, *Sociology in India: A Perspective from Sociology of Knowledge*, Jaipur, Rawat Publications, 1985.

Sheth, D.L., 'Globalization and New Politics of Micro-Movements', *Economic and Political Weekly*, Vol. 39, No. 1, 2004, pp. 45–58.

Shils, Edward, 'Scientific Development in the New States', in *Science and the New Nations*, New York (quoted from Bela Dutt Gupta, op. cit., p. XII), 1961.

Singh, Yogendra, 'The Scope and Method of Sociology in India and Sociology for India: The Emerging Perspective', in T.K.N. Unnithan et al. (eds), *Sociology for India*, Delhi, Prentice Hall, 1967.

——, *Modernization of Indian Tradition*, Delhi, Thompson Press, 1973.

——, 'Ideology, Theory, and Methods in Indian Sociology', in Stein Rokkan (ed.), *Quarter Century of International Social Science: Papers and Reports on Development*, 1952–1977, New Delhi, Concept Publishing Co., 1979.

——, *Indian Sociology: Social Conditioning and Emerging Concerns*, New Delhi, Vistar Publications, 1986.

——, *Ideology and Theory in Indian Sociology*, Jaipur, Rawat Publications, 2004.

——, 'Introduction', in Yogendra Singh (ed.), *Indian Sociology* (3 Vols.), ICSSR Research Surveys and Explorations, New Delhi, Oxford University Press, 2014, pp. 1–19.

Visvanathan, Shiv, 'Scripting Sociology of Science: Between Knowledge and Democracy in India', in Sujata Patel (ed.), op. cit., 2011, pp. 290–313.

CHAPTER 1

Some Issues in the Sociology of Knowledge

The question is not today whether sociology is science or art, and the question is also not of specific sociologies or specialisations. Now the questions are: How sociology has grown as a discipline? What constraints and challenges have been faced by it at various levels of its evolution? Comte emphasized positivism and evolutionism due to the constraint of achieving the status of a science for sociology.[1] Durkheim continued with the tradition of positivism with a view to establish superiority of society over individual.[2] Weber's plea for rationality-cum-subjectivity (interpretive understanding) for understanding society was influenced by socio-political condition in Germany.[3] The problems of English society due to industrialization influenced Marx's thinking, hence his dialectical historical materialism.[4] It is not to argue that only existential conditions of French, German and British societies influenced the thinking of Durkheim, Weber and Marx, the then thought-currents also played a great part in shaping their ideas.

Mill's idea of 'sociological imagination',[5] Berger's insistence on 'humanistic sociology',[6] Gouldner's conception of 'reflexive sociology',[7] and Rex and Wertheim's idea of 'emancipatory sociology'[8] refer to their reactions towards ideological implications of structural-functionalism and an alternative to the establishment sociology. The main thrust of their views is that reality should not be constructed mechanically. Construction of reality should refer to its social base and genesis. All constructions of reality imply idealizations, but the reality is not the same everywhere and in all situations, spatially and temporally.

It is necessary to detail the impact of theory upon social research, and to examine the impact of empirical situation upon theory. Merton has discussed the mutual bearing of theory and facts.[9] The researcher also effects research. His/her theoretical commitment not only influences his/her choice of a topic and statement of the problem, but it also often effects the selection of research procedures and the specific manner in which he/she analyses and disseminates his/her findings.[10] The researcher is a variable in the research design. No research could be examined without seeing the researcher's position in society and his/her ethical and political views. Research is not simply a technician's job. It involves ideology/philosophy (theory) on the one hand, and existent social situations on the other. Sociology of knowledge is an unavoidable element in social research.[11]

Weber's 'verstehen', Mead's 'take the role of the other' (empathy), Cooley's 'looking glass', and Goffman's 'dramaturgy' are some of the examples of the idealist/neo-idealist tradition.[12] A distinction is drawn between natural and social science researches, but the common points between the two are ignored. Historicism becomes a casualty with the idealists. The positivist tradition emphasizes the application of natural science model in social and cultural science researches. Comte was the first sociologist who advocated the idea of 'social physics' in sociology.[13] Lundberg advanced the principle of inertia in social research.[14] Carl Hempel talks of logical empiricism.[15] Thus, the emphasis is on attaining objective knowledge by sharing natural science logic of inquiry and research procedures. Thus, the positivists think of a mechanistic natural and social order.

The Sociology of Knowledge Perspective

'Sociology of knowledge ... seeks to analyse the relationship between knowledge and existence.'[16] Knowledge is related to social reality to discern its genesis. Role of historical and other forces could be seen to determine dynamics of knowledge vis-á-vis dynamics of society. Theory of knowledge or epistemology is a basic element of the sociology of knowledge. Theory of knowledge demands a certain level of consciousness for evaluation of the objects of perception. Stark mentions two varieties of the sociology of knowledge: (a) the macrosociology of knowledge, and (b) the microsociology of knowledge.[17] Merton, while making references about Mannheim and Sorokin, states: 'The sociology of knowledge takes on pertinence under a definite complex of social and cultural conditions.'[18] Merton, taking the diversity of formulations of Marx, Scheler, Durkheim, Mannheim, etc. proposes a paradigm for the sociology of knowledge. The main points of the paradigm are as follows:

1. Where is the existential basis of mental productions located?
    (a) Social bases.
    (b) Cultural bases.
2. What mental productions are being sociologically analysed?
    (a) Spheres of.
    (b) Which aspects are analysed?
3. How are mental productions related to the existential basis?
    (a) Causal as functional relations.
    (b) Symbolic or organismic or meaningful relations.
    (c) Ambiguous terms to designate relations.
4. Why are manifest and latent functions imputed to these existentially conditioned mental productions?
5. When do the imputed relations of the existential base and knowledge obtain?
    (a) Historicist theories.
    (b) General analytical theories.[19]

Merton discusses the main points of sociology of knowledge from Marx, Durkheim, Scheler and Mannheim. Marx refers to the superstructure as the existential basis of knowledge; Mannheim extends this basis as he talks of multiple group affiliation; Schelear speaks of a variety of forms of knowledge; and Durkheim explains the social genesis of thought. Merton's observation may be quoted here: 'A primary task of the sociology of knowledge is to discover the laws of transformation of these Weltanschauung'. And since these outlooks are by no means necessarily valid, it follows that the sociology of knowledge is not concerned merely with tracing the existential bases of truth but also of 'social illusion, superstition and socially conditioned errors and forms of deception.'[20]

Peter L. Berger and Thomas Luckmann consider their work – *The Social Construction of Reality* – as systematic, theoretical treatise in the sociology of knowledge. The foundations of knowledge are seen by them in 'everyday life.'[21] Their view is that reality is socially constructed and that the sociology of knowledge must analyse the process in which it occurs. Berger and Luckmann, while making a forceful plea for a phenomenological view of sociology of knowledge, write: 'A sociology of knowledge will have to deal not only with the empirical variety of knowledge in human societies, but also with the processes by which any body of "knowledge" comes to be socially established as "reality". The sociology of knowledge must concern itself with whatever passes for "knowledge" in a society, regardless of the ultimate validity (by whatever criteria) of such knowledge. All human knowledge is developed, transmitted and maintained in social situations. The sociology of knowledge is concerned with the analysis of the social construction of reality.'[22]

Like Marx and Mannheim, Berger and Luckmann accept existential determinism (social context) of thought. There are three roots of the sociology of knowledge: (a) the Marxian, (b) the Nietzschean and (c) the Historicist.[23] The approaches of Mannheim and Scheler are more of critiques of Marx's sociology of knowledge. Berger and Luckmann exclude epistemological and methodological problems from the sociology of knowledge. They consider the sociology of knowledge to be a part of the empirical discipline of sociology. However, their 'empiricism' is different from that of Talcott Parsons, R.K. Merton or C.W. Mills. They do not accept a positivist or a neo-positivist view of sociology of knowledge as phenomenology of Edmund Husserl emerged to begin with mainly as a strong reaction towards 'psychologism' in social sciences. They write: 'The sociology of knowledge must concern itself with everything that passes for knowledge in society'.[24]

Since phenomenology questions conventional sociological methodology, including positivism, neo-positivism and empiricism by highlighting problematiques in understanding of social phenomena, social reality or society, we are constrained to think whether or not phenomenology could be taken as an alternative position. At best, phenomenology provides a philosophical critique of the established conventions, methodology and empirical research. Phenomena are recognized and analysed in terms of their significance for members in the society. Meaningfulness is subjectively felt by the members, and this is realized by the phenomenologist. Hence, it remains at the level of description and interpretation in methodological terms. Obviously, phenomenology rejects the natural science paradigm, and as we know it that Husserl was basically against naturalistic and psychologistic explanations and exercises in human sciences. There is an attempt for externalization and objectification of the linguistic and cognitive world through accounts, understandings and analyses. This methodological exercise may be treated as an alternative to conventional sociology, but it is not without limitations. Consciousness and subjectivism still remain core concerns of phenomenological methodology. In a strict sense of the term, there is nothing like a phenomenological method of study as an alternative to the scientific method of study of the positivists. Phenomenology is a perspective, a theoretic orientation, hence does not accept reality in terms of its objective/subjective, macro/micro nature. Phenomenological understanding is empirical but not mechanical in nature.

Let us state that the phenomenological conception of the sociology of knowledge has not made inroads into theoretical and methodological domains of sociology in India. Mannheim and Scheler have also not made an impact on sociological researches in India. Marx, Weber and Durkheim and structural-functionalism of Parsons and Merton and functionalism of Radcliffe-Brown have made their imprints on Indian sociology. Of late, neo-Marxist thinking and neo-positivist orientation have been talked about mainly at the level of teaching in the classrooms. Therefore, we shall give a brief resume of Marx, Durkheim and Weber's sociology of knowledge.

Sociology of Knowledge: Marx, Durkheim and Weber

Economic and Philosophic Manuscripts of 1844 by Karl Marx analyses private property and labour, private property and communism, and the power of money in bourgeois society.[25] It also provides a critical analysis of Hegelian dialectic and Hegelian philosophy as a whole. Emphasis is laid on the 'estrangement of labour', or the 'alienation of the labourer' in capitalist society.[26] In the Hegelian philosophy, the category of 'estrangement' is prominently found; it is also seen in Feuerbach's philosophic criticism of religion. Hegel speaks of the alienation of self-consciousness and Feuerbach of the alienation of the abstract, non-historical and non-class man. Marx speaks of the 'estrangement' or 'alienation' of the labourer. Marx gives an entirely new economic, class and historical content to the conception of 'estrangement'. 'By "estrangement" or "alienation" Marx means the forced labour of the labourer for the capitalist, the appropriation by the capitalist of the product of a worker's labour and the separation of the labourer from the means of production, confront the labourer as an alien, enslaving power.'[27]

Peter Hamilton observes: 'The concept of alienation is as central to what constitutes Marx's sociology of knowledge as it is to his work as a whole.'[28] Hamilton further writes: 'Alienation expresses how the relationship between the material basis of life-work and man's conception of himself as a social being is distorted, to produce in capitalist societies a reification of social relations, a reduction of their human nature to the status of things, as mere objects'.[29] Marx shows that the worker sinks to the level of commodity and becomes indeed the most wretched of commodities. Marx observes: 'The worker becomes all the poorer the more wealth he produces, the more his production increases in power and size'.[30] Marx speaks of the devaluation of the world of men in direct proportion to the increasing value of the world of things. Labour produces itself and the worker as a commodity. Labour's product confronts it as *something alien,* as a power independent of the producer.

The following two quotations from *Economic and Philosophic Manuscripts of 1844* clearly bring out alienation of labour as the basis of Marx's sociology of knowledge:

1. 'The product of labour is labour which has been embodied in an object, which has become material: it is the objectification

of labour. Labour's realization is its *objectification.* Under these economic conditions this realization of labour appears as *loss of realisation* for the workers; objectification as *loss of the object and bondage to it;* appropriation as *estrangement,* as *alienation*'.[31]

2. 'Whatever the product of his labour is, he is not. Therefore, the greater this product, the less is he himself. The alienation of the worker in his product means not only that his labour becomes an object, an external existence, but it exists outside him, independently, as something alien to him, and that it becomes a power on its own confronting him. It means that the life which he has conferred on the object confronts him as something hostile and alien'.[32]

Thus, Marx speaks of the *objectification* of the labour. Labour is externalized. Worker exists as an object of labour, and as a physical subject. Direct relation of the worker with his labour is concealed by political economy. The alienation of labour constitutes: (a) labour is external to the worker, (b) there is self-estrangement, and (c) man is a species-being, that is, life becomes a means for him. Marx's sociology of knowledge is evident in the following statement:

> The worker produces capital, capital produces him – hence he produces himself, and man as worker, as a commodity is the product of this entire cycle.[33]

Marx states that foreignness of man and capital is *real.* He further states: 'The worker exists as a worker only when he exists for himself as capital; and he exists as capital only when some capital exists for him. The existence of capital is his existence, his life, as it determines the tenor of his life in a manner indifferent to him'.[34]

Marx and Engels expressed their reaction to the Hegelian notion of ideology and provided their own view about it in the German Ideology,[35] a monumental work. Marx has attacked the mysticism of the Hegelian philosophy. Under Hegelian philosophy, the dominance of religion was taken for granted. Every dominant relationship was pronounced as a religious relationship and transformed into a cult, a cult of law, a cult of the state, etc. On all sides, it was only a question of dogmas and beliefs in dogmas, conceptions, thoughts, ideas; and all the products of consciousness were considered as existing, independent of man's existence. Marx and Engels, while rejecting the Hegelian view about knowledge, observe that men produce their means of subsistence, their actual material life. This is what they call – 'the mode of production'. The mode of production, in fact, refers to a definite form of activity, of life, of individuals. 'As individuals express their life, so they are. What they are, therefore, coincides with their production, both with what they produce and with how they produce. The nature of individuals thus depends on the material conditions determining their production'.[36]

Thus, all conceptions, thoughts, ideas and consciousness come from the existence of man in relation to nature and other men. We would like to reproduce the following statements of Marx and Engels from *The German Ideology* in regard to their sociology of knowledge:

> The production of ideas, of conceptions, of consciousness, is at first directly interwoven with the material activity and the material intercourse of men, the language of real life. Conceiving, thinking, the mental intercourse of men, appear at this stage as the direct efflux (result) of their material behaviour. The same applies to mental production as expressed in the language of politics, laws, morality, religion, metaphysics, etc. of a people. Men are the producers of their conceptions, ideas, etc. real, active men, as they are conditioned by a definite development of their productive forces and of their intercourse corresponding to these, up to its furthest forms. Consciousness can never be anything else than conscious existence, and the existence of men is their actual life-process.[37]

'In direct contrast to German Philosophy, which descends from heaven to earth, here we ascend from earth to heaven. That is to say, we do not set out from what men say, imagine, conceive, nor from men as narrated, thought of, imagined, conceived, in order to arrive at men in the flesh. We set out from real, active men, and on the basis of their real life process we demonstrate the development of the ideological reflexes and echoes of this life process. Morality, religion, metaphysics, all the rest of ideology and their corresponding forms of consciousness, thus no longer retain the semblance of independence. They have no history, no development; but men, developing their material production and their material intercourse, alter, along with this their real existence, their thinking, and the products of their thinking. Life is not determined by consciousness, but consciousness by life.'[38]

Thus, it is the consciousness of individuals themselves, their real life and process of development of men which are the basis of Marx's construction of concepts and categories. Marx has a juxtaposition of science and ideology. Marx was interested in understanding of the distortions of consciousness exemplified in ideology. He was interested in knowing existential basis of ideology and its justification of the interests of dominant classes. Social determinism of ideas is Marx's fundamental contribution to the sociology of knowledge.

Emile Durkheim provides an alternative approach to the study of sociology of knowledge in comparison to Karl Marx's theory of knowledge and ideology.[39] Hamilton observes a fundamental tension in Durkheimian writings, between determinism and voluntarism, and between positivism and idealism. This tension is due to Durkheim's methodological orientation and his conceptualization of society and the 'sociale'.[40] Methodologically, Durkheim combined positivism and empiricism and society receives its first systematic conceptualization as a collective representation. Religion is a substantive reality for Durkheim. Durkheim's positivistic methodology is due to this understanding of religion. Religion is a social fact, its social existence is irrefutable. It is true, and therefore, expresses human needs and human existence. Thus, Durkheim's positivism and organicism have clearly ideological overtones. Durkheim's ontology about religion is correlated with his methodology. However, Durkheim's sociology of knowledge is different from Marx's in the sense that 'social' for Durkheim does not mean 'material facts'. For Marx, 'material facts' are social. Durkheim is an empiricist and not a deductionist. But Durkheim has non-empirical assumptions about social solidarity, collective representations and religion.

Max Weber incorporates the ideas of both Marx and Nietzsche. With Marx, Weber shares the sociological approaches to ideas: they are powerless in history unless they are fused with material interests.[41] With Nietzsche, Weber is deeply concerned with the importance of ideas for psychic reactions. However, Weber refuses to conceive of ideas being mere reflections of psychic or social interests. He sees tensions between ideas and interests. For Weber, there is no 'correspondence', 'reflection' or 'expression' between ideas and interests, individualism and organicism, holism and idealism.

In Durkheim, organicism is tempered by positivism as it is evident in his classics – *The Rules of Sociological Method and Division of Labour in Society*. Later on, organicism overwhelms positivism as it is evidenced in another work – *The Elementary Forms of the Religious Life*. Durkheim's theory is known as 'correspondence theory of knowledge'. 'Mechanical solidarity', 'collective consciousness' and 'organic solidarity' and needs of groups and individuals must be seen in this context. Super-individual and functionally coercive reality are seen in social phenomena.

Knowledge for Durkheim does not exist apart from the social existence of men, and society is seen as having an external power over men, and it is real only in so far as it exists in the collective consciousness. Thus, knowledge, beliefs, ideas are simply aspects of that collective consciousness, whose basis is the form of society itself. In this way, concepts and categories of understanding are not apriori, but are created by the facts of social life. Ideas are constructed as representations of social organization in terms of its collective nature. Society is treated by Durkheim as a moral collectivity. Analysis of the social conditions of knowledge must logically proceed from an understanding of the way in which there is 'collective affinity'. Marx and Weber stand quite opposite to Durkheimian Sociology of knowledge.

For Marx, interests express ideas. For Weber, they are a matter of 'affinity', 'a point of coincidence', or 'convergence'. The content of ideas and their origin are separate entities. Ideas have autonomous role in present capitalism but certainly not in Hegelian sense. 'World images' are created by ideas. These represent social conditions of specific strata.

Weber considers ideologies as notions that justify and motivate materially interested strata. 'Wherever interests are vigorously pursued, an ideology tends to be developed also to give meaning, reinforcement and justification to these interests. And this ideology is as "real" as the real interests themselves, for ideology is an indispensable part of the life-process which is expressed in action. And conversely, whenever ideas are to conquer the world, they require the leverage of real interests, although frequently ideas will more or less detract these interests from their original aim'.[42] It is evident that Max Weber tried to have a mix of the Marxian, the materialist and the psychological traditions of thinking. The socio-political conditions of Germany of that time also demanded such a construction or frame of reference for understanding human society. However, Weber also reacted sharply by working out such a frame to the then existing streams of thinking.

Not only Marx brought out an 'epistemological break', Durkheim and Weber also provided alternative constructions to Marx's epistemology. Now the question is: Whether these thinkers created more mystification about understanding of society or they ensured a sort of demystification of earlier mystifications given by Hegel, Nietzsche, etc.? All neologisms create mystifications and task of sociology is to demystify the world. It is to deal with both phenomenal and noumenal man.[43] Gouldner claims to demystify the establishment sociology by his *reflective sociology*.[44]

Positivism and Sociology of Knowledge

Paradigms and constructs become a base for sociology of knowledge. However, paradigms may have their genesis in mental as well as existential conditions of the society. Karl R. Popper's view is that historicism is a poor method. Logically speaking, it is impossible to predict the future course of history. In his well-known work – *The Poverty of Historicism*, Popper makes the following statements:

1. The course of human history is strongly influenced by the growth of human knowledge.
2. We can not predict, by rational or scientific methods, the future growth of our scientific knowledge.

3. We cannot, therefore, predict the future course of human history.
4. Hence, there is no possibility of a theoretical history, of a historical social science or historical prediction.
5. The historical method is thus a misconception.[45]

While the methods of the natural sciences are fundamentally nominalistic, social science must adopt a methodological essentialism. Social sciences cannot benefit from naturalism or scientism. Popper talks of generalizations confined to the concrete historical period in which the relevant observations are made. Thus, both logic and empiricism remain hallmarks of Popper's view. Popper does not approve of historicism, Hegelianism and Marxism. He talks of 'indeterminism' of the past as well as of future, but gives premium to the present alone.

The debate on positivism has been quite widespread during the 1960s and the 1970s in Europe, and particularly in Germany. Its basic features are referred as (a) methodological monism or unity of scientific method, (b) the exact sciences as a methodological ideal for all other sciences, and (c) causal scientific explanation.[46] A counter to this view was provided by Karl Marx in *The German Ideology*. Marx writes: 'We know only a single science, the science of history. History can be contemplated from two sides, it can be divided into the history of nature and the history of mankind. However, the sides are not to be divided off; as long as men exist, the history of nature and the history of men are mutually conditioned'.[47] The attempt is clearly made out by the positivists to separate the natural from the historical or social and cultural. Marx gives premium to the latter and at the same time brings out the interdependence of the two. However, Popper and his followers have given a theory of method, independent of a social theory and the former being in fact a theory of scientific and philosophical nature. Thus, the question is: Can knowledge and apparatus of knowledge accumulation be independent of the existence of society which utilizes knowledge and its products? Popper does not touch upon this sort of question. Logic and mechanics of method are essentials of Popper's thinking. Instrumentality of science is, therefore, the core of Popper's view.

We do not propose to provide a variety of criticisms of Popper's view. However, Thomas S. Kuhn's – *The Structure of Scientific Revolution* brings out the role of history in scientific development and accumulation of knowledge.[48] Historical studies suggest the possibility of a new image of science. Normal science also becomes a constraint on development of fundamental novelties in the realm of knowledge. 'Normal science means research firmly based upon one or more past scientific achievements, that some particular scientific community acknowledges for a time as supplying the foundation for its further practice'.[49]

Kuhn talks of transformations of the paradigms as scientific revolutions. These transformations from one paradigm to another via revolution is the usual developmental pattern of natural science. History of science is the only way to understand this change and transformation of knowledge. Kuhn writes: 'A paradigm is what the members of a scientific community share, and, conversely, a scientific community consists of men who share a paradigm.'[50] He further observes: 'A scientific community consists, on this view, of the practitioners of a scientific speciality.'[51] Paradigms are puzzle solving. They refer to the pre-paradigm period, its emergence and maturation and post-paradigm phase. It is this history of science in relation to the conditions of society which becomes a real guide for generation of knowledge. Both normal science and revolutions are thus community-based activities.[52]

A sociology of knowledge perspective must consider the following points: (a) epistemology – theory of the acquisition of knowledge, (b) philosophy – substantive worldview, (c) theory – substantive hypotheses to account for their object of study, (d) methodology – lower level prescriptions as to *method,* and (e) field of study – actual object of study.[53] Now, the question is: How far Mannheim's relationism and existentialism have been taken up for understanding Indian society? Whether Parsons' functionalism has been adopted in view of the above mentioned five points or it has been accepted due to academic colonialism of Western social science? Marx's theories of social classes, state, his analysis of culture, the Marxist anthropology and methodology are to be seen in Indian context from the point of the five points mentioned above. The same is the case with Radcliffe-Brownian functionalism in regard to its naturalistic, empiricist and comparative elements. Variants of positivism have been reflected in empirical and analytical writings on Indian society.

Notes

1. Cf. W. Stark, *The Sociology of Knowledge,* London: Routledge & Kegan Paul, 1977, pp. 157–60. Also see, 'Society and Government', by August Comte, reprinted from the *Positive Philosophy* in *Theories of Society* (ed.) Talcott Parsons et al., The Free Press, 1961, pp. 125–38.
2. Emile Durkheim, *The Elementary Forms of the Religious Life* (Paperback), London: George Allen & Unwin Ltd., 1976.
3. Reinhard Bendix, *Max Weber. An Intellectual Portrait,* Berkeley: University of California Press (Paperback), 1977, pp. 30–41.
4. Karl Marx and Frederick Engels, *The German Ideology,* Moscow: Progress Publishers, 1968.
5. C. Wright Mills, *The Sociological Imagination,* Penguin Books, 1971.
6. Peter L. Berger, *Invitation to Sociology,* Penguin Books, 1971.
7. Alvin W. Gouldner, *The Coming Crisis of Western Sociology,* London: Heinemann Educational Books Ltd., 1971, pp. 488–500.
8. See John Rex, *Sociology and the Demystification of the Modern World,* London: Routledge & Kegan Paul, 1974, pp. 3–33; and W.F. Wertheim, *Evolution and Revolution: The Rising Waves of Emancipation,* Penguin Books, 1974, pp. 35–62.
9. Robert K. Merton, *Social Theory and Social Structure,* Glencoe: The Free Press, 1962, pp. 85–117.
10. S. Sjoberg and R. Nett, *A Methodology for Social Research,* New York: Harper and Row Publishers, 1968, pp. 2–3.
11. Ibid., pp. 4–10.
12. See, for example, Max Weber, *The Theory of Social and Economic Organization,* Glencoe: The Free Press, 1947, pp. 112–23; George H. Mead, *Mind Self and Society,* Chicago: Chicago University Press, 1934, pp. 253–57. C.H. Cooley., *Social Organization,* Glencoe: The Free Press, 1956, pp. 23–31; and E. Goffman, *The Presentation of Self in Everyday Life,* Penguin Books, 1956.
13. A. Comte, op. cit.
14. George A. Lundberg, *Social Research,* New York: Longman, 1942.

15. C.G. Hempel and P. Oppenheim, 'The Logic of explanation', in H. Feigl and M. Brodbeck (eds) *Readings in the Philosophy of Sciences,* New York: Appleton-Century-Crofts; 1953, pp. 319–352.
16. Karl Mannheim, *Ideology and Utopia,* London: Routledge and Kegan Paul 1960, p. 237.
17. W. Stark, op. cit., pp. 19–37.
18. Robert K. Merton, op. cit., p. 457.
19. Ibid., pp. 460–461.
20. Ibid., p. 470.
21. Peter L. Berger and Thomas Luckmann, *The Social Construction of Reality,* Penguin Books, 1972.
22. Ibid., p. 15.
23. Ibid., p. 17.
24. Ibid., p. 26. See also, Max Scheler, *Problems of a Sociology of Knowledge* (Translated by M.S. Frings and edited by K.W. Stikkers), London: Routledge and Kegan Paul, 1980.
25. Karl Marx, *Economic and Philosophic Manuscripts of 1884,* Moscow: Progress Publishers, 1974.
26. Ibid., p. 7.
27. Ibid., p. 18.
28. Peter Hamilton, *Knowledge and Social Structure,* London: Routledge and Kegan Paul, 1974, p. 19.
29. Ibid., p. 19.
30. Karl Marx, op. cit., 1974, p. 63.
31. Ibid., p. 63.
32. Ibid., p. 64.
33. Ibid., p. 75.
34. Ibid., p. 75.
35. Karl Marx and Frederick Engels, op. cit., 1968.
36. Ibid., p. 32.
37. Ibid., p. 37.
38. Ibid., pp. 37–38.
39. See Emile Durkheim, op. cit., 1976.
40. Peter Hamilton, op. cit., pp. 103–119.
41. Max Weber, *From Max Weber. Essays in Sociology,* (edited by H.H. Gerth and C. Wright-Mills), London: Routledge and Kegan Paul (Paperback), 1970, pp. 45–74.
42. Ibid., p. 47.

43. John Rex, op. cit., 1974.
44. A.W. Gouldner, op. cit., 1971.
45. Karl R. Popper, *The Poverty of Historicism,* London: Routledge and Kegan Paul (Paperback), 1979, p. 30.
46. David Frisby, 'An introduction to the English translation', *The Positivist Dispute in German Sociology* (ed.), London: Heinemann, 1976, p. xii. This volume contains contributions by Adorno, Albert, Dahrendorf, Habermas, Pilot and Popper. The debate on positivism vs historicism has been analysed in detail in this volume. Popper's other writings have been consulted by us, but we have referred here only *The Poverty of Historicism.*
47. Ibid., p. xvi.
48. Thomas S. Kuhn, *The Structure of Scientific Revolutions,* Chicago: The Chicago University Press, 1962.
49. Ibid., p. 10.
50. Ibid., p. 176.
51. Ibid., p. 177.
52. Ibid., p. 179.
53. Miriam Glucksmann, 'The structuralism of Levi-Strauss and Althusser', in John Rex (ed.), *Approaches to Sociology,* London: Routledge & Kegan Paul, 1974, p. 232.

Chapter 2

Sociology in India

Historical and Theoretic Probings

Now, the question is about the nature of Indian sociology – its theories, concepts and methodology. A number of points could be discussed about Indian sociology in relation to its founding fathers, namely, G.S. Ghurye, Radhakamal Mukerjee and D.P. Mukerji. Other sociologists who have contributed significantly to the evolution of Indian sociology are A.K. Saran, Ramkrishna Mukherjee, A.R. Desai, I.P. Desai, K.M. Kapadia, M.N. Srinivas, Y. Singh, Andre Beteille, T.N. Madan, etc. from among the Indian sociologists. Both British and American sociologists have conducted researches in India. We shall also analyse their influence on Indian sociology. Louis Dumont, a French anthropologist, alone has influenced Indian sociology to a considerable extent. The important questions to be inquired are:

1. What is the 'fit' between theory, method and data in Indian sociology?
2. What are the ideological influences on the understanding of Indian society?
3. How to construct social reality in the Indian context?
4. Could there be an Indian sociology different from sociologies of other countries/societies?

Other questions are: What is the input of the idealist and the positivist traditions in Indian sociology? How far has it been useful in constructing India's social reality? How and why the two traditions have been accepted for studying Indian society? What is the role of the Marxist tradition in studying Indian society?

Early Theoretic and Methodological Concerns

A crucial question is: What are ontological and methodological assumptions of Indian sociology? Theory and methodology refer to the sociology of knowledge perspective, that is, the way the reality of Indian sociology has been understood. The early phase of Indian sociology was clearly led by G.S. Ghurye on the one hand, and Radhakamal Mukerjee on the other. Ghurye had no clear theoretical perspective and methodological orientation, but he was influenced by the British diffusionism due to his association with Rivers. Ghurye's early studies were of Indological nature. However, Ghurye had a lot of catholicity in guiding research to his students as he allowed them to work on a variety of themes with varied theoretical and methodological orientations. Ghurye's interest in Indological data speaks of his ontological orientation. Ghurye has provided a sort of 'philosophical anthropology', which is implicit in his analysis of Indian social structure.

Radhakamal Mukerjee talks of universal categories and concepts. According to Mukerjee, sociology could be a universal social science, and it should be related to natural and other social sciences.[1] Mukerjee finds both the Western liberal democratic pattern and the Marxist models inadequate. He integrates social science model at a meta-scientific and meta-anthropological level. It is a 'human general theory of relativity' that resolves the conflict between the philosophy of science and the philosophy of values. Mukerjee's explanations are based on deductive reasoning, hence exogenous and speculative.

Thus, sociology in India has been guided from its inception by the particularistic as well as universalistic criteria. At Lucknow University, Mukerjee advocated a universalistic brand of sociology. A.K. Saran takes an extreme view as he rejects the sociology produced in the West as a response to the forces of industrialization. D.P. Mukerji prefers historical-dialectical mode of sociological analysis rather than empirical-positivistic one. D.P. Mukerji rejects atomism and modern methods of research. He accepts an Indianized version of the Marxian approach.[2] Thus,

Mukerji is found in the middle of the positions taken by Radhakamal Mukerjee and A.K. Saran.

Similar differences in theoretical and methodological orientations existed among the sociologists at the Bombay University. Ghurye represented a particularistic view though different from A.K. Saran's approach. Ghurye's students, K.M. Kapadia and I. Karve, followed Ghurye's methodological position with certain modifications. However, A.R. Desai strongly advocated the orthodox Marxist approach in his study of Indian nationalism, village community, peasant movements and the Indian state.

Marx, Durkheim and Weber, the founding fathers of sociology are taught in Indian universities as a major part of a course on thinkers and sociological theory. Talcott Parsons and Robert K. Merton are also taught along with B. Malinowski and Radcliffe-Brown. It is not to say that thinkers representing American, British, German, French and other countries are not taught, but these three founding fathers and some prominent representatives of American and British sociology are generally taught in all departments of sociology at postgraduate level. Their sociological thinking has influenced immensely the students and teachers of sociology in India. We shall bring this point home in our analysis of Indian sociology.

B.D. Gupta observes that the story of Indian sociology has not been properly told. The late arrival of sociology in India is wrongly attributed to the philosophical and religious orientations of Indian intellectuals.[3] Max Mueller, Emile Senart, C. Bougie, Max Weber, P.A. Sorokin and E. Shils, etc. condemned Indian sociology for not studying material interests. Indian sociology is blamed for accepting 'adaptive' researches and 'routinized' science, which required no original thinking or creativity.[4] Gupta observes that Indology and religio-philosophic thinking influenced R.N. Saxena, A.K. Saran and Y.B. Damle. Indian sociologists have been characterised as 'tradition-bound' and as the advocates of the study of 'subjective' values and 'pattern maintenance'. Y. Singh has been referred as having said that Indian sociology has remained limited in its scope, approaches and procedures. 'Positivism' was found lacking in Indian sociology in the pre-independence period.

Gupta considers the above comments on Indian sociology as 'partial, one-sided and prejudiced'. She writes: 'It shows a lack of knowledge and understanding too, of the local history and of the indigenous developments of institutions. It is not true that there was any built-in reluctance or resistance among intellectuals in India in the eighteenth and nineteenth centuries to take natural science as the paradigm of human knowledge.'[5] Gupta refers to the establishment of the Asiatic Society in 1784 and a host of other institutions later on. She observes that social and religious prejudices did not stand in the way of accepting natural science as the paradigm of human knowledge. Certainly, British colonialism largely determined the intellectual climate and scientific temperament in India in the 19th century.

Sociology in India has its claim for emergence from the middle of the 19th century. 'In that, "sociology" in the West and in India is almost contemporaneous'.[6] Sociological reflection and research existed even before the middle of the 19th century. Sociology is not a post–1947 phenomenon, thriving in 'borrowed plumes', and sociology in India had a secular basis. Gupta talks of 'a sociology of sociology'. She formulates the following questions in this regard: (a) Is there a tradition of sociological thinking and some primary accumulation of sociological knowledge in this country? What indeed was the intellectual potentiality of receiving the science of society in India? (b) What were the broad historical, social and cultural factors that shaped the birth and development of sociology, both in its reflectional and actional aspects in India? (c) What was the receptivity or the association of social networks, like institutions, associations, personal contacts within which sociological thinking and empirical researches were promoted? A common answer to these questions would be that 'philosophical thought about society as a whole and an attempt to carry out secular solution of social problems characterized the early precursors of sociology in India.'[7] But Gupta talks more of social welfare, social policy and social action oriented understanding of Indian society and research in the 19th century. The formalization of sociology as a discipline for teaching and research at university level is a phenomenon of the late 1920s.

Prevalence of consciousness among intellectuals about India's problems could not be equalled with sensitization and conscientization of sociology as a discipline. Raja Ram Mohan Roy had understanding of India's social problems, but he was not a professional sociologist. Colonialism had its impact on Bengal more than any other state in the early phase, hence development of social science and sociology in Bengal. Sir Brijendranath Seal advocated the use of 'comparative sociology', and strongly refuted the relevance of the British anthropology and the American ethnology for understanding Indian society. Seal had anti-evolutionism and anti-Western thinking for the singular cause of the defence of Indian culture. A sense of national pride was part of Seal's thinking. Radhakamal Mukerjee rejected the western individualistic conception of man and social order and also the Marxist view of class and class-conflict. He advanced the new idea of collectivity, namely, Sangha. D.P. Mukerji emphasized the Indianization of the Marxist approach and *indigenization* of understanding of India's social reality. He rejected the Western idea of empiricism and advocated the cause of *interpretive method* for sociology in India. This certainly promoted *methodological particularism*, but, in fact, it did not emerge as an alternative to the Western approaches and methodologies. Dumont's approach is a variant of methodological particularism.

Time and again, the question about the nature of sociology in India has been put forth by sociologists from abroad as well as from within the country. The debate was carried in the writings of Radhakamal Mukerjee, D.P. Mukerji and A.K. Saran. Later on, in the late 1950s L. Dumont and D.F. Pocock[8] took up the debate with the publication of the *Contributions to Indian Sociology* in 1957. The debate even today continues in the pages of the *Contributions to Indian Sociology*, New Series. F.G. Bailey, T.N. Madan, J.P.S. Uberoi, D. Narain, Y. Singh, I. Ahmad and some others joined the debate on the issue.[9] A couple of articles also appeared in *Sociological Bulletin*,[10] particularly with reference to teaching of and research in Sociology in Indian universities and colleges. Two seminars were conducted in the 1960s – one at Agra (U.P.), and the other at Mount Abu (Rajasthan). The proceedings of the two seminars are available in print – *Sociology in India*[11] and *Sociology for India*,[12] respectively.

The issue was: Whether sociology in India should be a part of global sociology or it should have Indianness in its concepts, categories, classifications, approaches and methods of research investigations? Protagonists of both the views are found in these two volumes.

Later on, Ramkrishna Mukherjee brought out a volume – *Trends in Indian Sociology*. Y. Singh has provided a scheme of analysis for Indian sociology in a couple of essays.[13] We shall refer to their views in a chronological order in our analysis. Here, we intend to highlight only the salient features of this debate. The details of the debate will be taken up in another chapter. It may be noted that the sociologists who have been engaged in the debate on the nature of sociology in India are not of the Marxist disposition. D.P. Mukerji was the only one who called himself a 'Marxologist', rather than a Marxist. He was interested in development of sociology in India from the point of its historicity and structure of tradition.

Universal vs Specific Sociology for India

Now, let us take up proceedings of the two seminars on sociology in India, held in the 1960s. R.N. Saxena, Y.B. Damle, Y. Singh, B.R. Chauhan and Indra Deva are contributors to both the volumes. However, R.N. Saxena has expressed the same view in several addresses and papers which he holds in the volumes: *Sociology in India* and *Sociology for India*. The other well- known names are Victor S. D'Souza, K.M. Kapadia and K.C. Panchanadikar and J.M. Panchanadikar. None of these scholars, with the exception of Y. Singh, have joined the debate on Indian sociology in the pages of *Contributions to Indian Sociology*.

An Indological or culturological approach has been the hallmark of several sociologists. They have hammered on against the acceptance of theoretical and methodological orientations of the Western countries. These scholars emphasize on the role of traditions, and group rather than individual as the basis of social relations, and advocate religion, ethics and philosophy as the basis of social organisations. R.N. Saxena, for example, stresses on the role of the concepts of Dharma, Artha, Kamma and Moksha.[14] Dumont and Pocock emphasize on utility of the Indological sources for sociological formulations.[15] Saxena observes that sociology in the Indian universities has been shaped on the Western pattern.[16] The Western sociology is no doubt 'empirical' and 'positivistic', but it fails to provide a proper examination of spiritual values and other super-nonempirical ideas. After arguing a case for the relevance of the study of categorical values and norms, Saxena writes: 'A correct approach to Indian sociology can only be a synthesis of empiricism and intuition and a proper recognition of the fact that spiritual values have an important role in our social life.'[17]

Indra Deva discerns the following points which might make a reference to the term 'Indian sociology':

1. A body of concepts and generalizations applicable specifically to Indian society and culture;
2. sociological principles derived from traditional Indian sources;
3. the study of social structure and social processes in India; and
4. sociology as it has developed in India.[18]

However, these points are not exclusive when they are used for denoting 'Indian sociology'. After having discussed these points, Indra Deva formulates a view contrary to that of Saxena. He observes that though Indian society has some features of its own, the distinctiveness about it is not so fundamental as to necessitate the development of an 'Indian sociology' in the sense of special conceptual and theoretical framework. The task is to develop the general sociological theories, concepts and methodology, which can be applicable to a premodern, mainly peasant society, like India. Ananda K. Coomaraswamy talked of the essential unity of all traditional societies.[19] In other words, such societies would represent a social formation different from that of the Western industrialized societies. Deva suggests that western ethnocentrism must go from the existing theoretical and conceptual framework of sociology, and a theoretical system be evolved which can do justice to the structural, functional and the dynamic aspects of the Indian society.[20]

Y.B. Damle is very particular in regard to sociology in India. He writes: 'In order to take cognizance of both stability and change, I would suggest the use of the Parsonian frame of reference for the study of Indian sociology.'[21] Parson's view that personality, culture and society are 'atomistic' as well as interdependent systems and constitute the social system is explained by Damle as relevant for studying Indian society. Damle observes: 'Talking in terms of functional prerequisites one finds in India that greatest amount of premium is put on pattern maintenance rather than on adaptation and goal attainment.'[22] Later on, Damle adopted Merton's theory of 'reference group' for analysing social mobility in the caste system in India.[23] Damle suggests a paradigm adopted from Parsons for application to the analysis of social system in India. It is concluded by Damle that no special theory is needed for studying Indian sociology.[24]

Western Social Science and Sociology in India

Y. Singh proposes three points relevant to the disciplinary growth of sociology in India: (a) the changing historico-political status of the country; (b) the changing nature of western intellectual contact and its vicissitudes, and (c) the native intellectual traditions from which the sociologists themselves emerged.[25] In the first phase, Indian social structure, values and institutions were analysed but not as a response to the Western social science. The second phase refers to the combination of empirical and historico-philosophical analysis of Radhakamal Mukerjee, and the application of a Marxologist approach to the study of Indian society, its tradition, culture and class structure by D.P. Mukerji. The microstatic studies by B. Malinowski and R. Brown replaced the macro-dynamic studies in Britain at the time when the two Mukerjees were busy in giving a sound shape to Indian sociology. With the freedom of India, the era of sponsored researches started in India. However, the researches funded by the Western countries were also carried out in the 1950s and 1960s in India on a bigger scale.

Thus, the ideology of the Government on the one hand, and the ideology of the Western social science on the other, simultaneously influenced social research in the first two decades of India's independence. Singh states that (a) increased quantification and abstracted empiricism, (b) increased experimentalism, and (c) greater arbitrariness in regard to concepts and definitions are the significant trends of sociology as a discipline in India.[26] Sociology in India in the early 1960s is characterized by functionalism and neofunctionalism, historical comparative method and logico-philosophical and symbolic methods of analysis.[37] 'Thus, anti-positivism and functionalism, positivism and logico-philosophical orientations influenced Indian sociologists simultaneously in the 1950s and 1960s. The Western "scientism" could not overtake Indian sociology completely, it remained in India also as a philosophy of society and history'.[28] Singh prefers to have a synthesis of sociological empiricism and analytical quality of vision.

In two essays (a) 'Scope and Method of Sociology in India', and (b) 'Sociology for India: The Emerging Perspective', in *Sociology for India*, Y. Singh exemplifies his own view and the resume of the above Seminar, respectively. Some of the points mentioned in the Agra Seminar have been repeated by Singh in the first paper of the above seminar. Singh writes: 'Sociology in India or the whole university culture in this country has been an extension of the Western, primarily the British tradition. Growing American influence is a post-independence phenomenon.'[29] Colonialism created academic and intellectual parasitism and regression. The pre-independence sociology could be characterized by descriptive, evolutionary, analytical and comparative studies and by particularism of Indian society and culture. However, Singh notes that both the organismic positivism and mechanistic positivism of the 19th century European sociology were absent in Indian sociology, and even some sociologists strongly reacted and refuted them.[30]

The post-independence sociology could be characterized by (a) the comparative historical approach, (b) philosophico-sociological approach, (c) logico-philosophical approach, (d) structural-functional approach, and (e) statistical-positivistic approach.[31] Researches by G.S. Ghurye and K.M. Kapadia fall in the first approach. A.R. Desai has been put with Ghurye and Kapadia as a variant of the comparative historical approach with emphasis on historical-dialectical materialism. Three variants of philosophico-sociological approach are represented by Radhakamal Mukerjee and D.P. Mukerji. A.K. Saran represents the logico-philosophical approach. We have mentioned earlier that with the Lucknow school of sociology, R.K.M. and A.K.S. represented two extremes and D.P.M. occupied the middle position.

M.N. Srinivas, S.C. Dube, D.N. Majumdar and McKim Marriott may be considered as representatives of the structural-functional approach (both the variants – the British and the American). Many more names could be associated with this approach including that of F.G. Bailey, Louis Dumont, Y. Singh, Andre Beteille, Rajni Kothari, Anil Bhatt, etc. representing its variants. Y. Singh finds that this approach has contributed to the enrichment of sociology in India as a *scientific discipline* (emphasis added). The statistical-positivistic approach has been applied in conducting surveys and studies of urban and industrial situations. Singh does not refer names, but we could certainly refer to V.S. D'Souza, Ramkrishna Mukherjee, Anil Bhatt and some others who have carried out urban surveys and applied statistical tests. Y. Singh has applied such an approach in his study of the teachers of Rajasthan University.[32]

Y. Singh mentions Dumont and Pocock's view about Indian sociology and questions its theoretic position. He writes: 'In my view, the approach of these writers remains by and large structural and functional.'[33] Further, he says that it is closer to Levi-Strauss' *structuralism* and Durkheim's *functionalism,* rather than Radcliffe-Brown's functionalism. 'Consensual', 'manipulative' and 'alienative' approaches and researches have been referred by Edward Shils in a quite demeaning manner. However, Y. Singh observes 'consensus' in structural-functional approach, 'alienation' in the comparative-historical and philosophico-sociological approaches, and 'manipulation' in structural-positivistic sociology.[34]

Y. Singh discusses L. Dumont and D.F. Pocock's view in *Sociology for India* in somewhat detail. He concludes: 'The task for construction of a sociology for India then will be to establish parallels and correspondences between the general and specific levels of sociological aspects.'[35] Further, Singh writes: 'Hence our conclusion is twofold: (a) Sociology would include both the study of Indian culture and social structure through adaptation of conceptual categories of general sociology to specific problems encountered in Indian situation, and (b) this may not and should not imply a methodological particularism or disciplinary isolation.'[36] Thus, Singh does not find a polarity or opposition between a sociology for India and a general theory of sociology.

Indigenization of Sociology in India

Let us now refer to the objectives and discussions of the seminar held at Mount Abu. The objectives are mentioned as follows in the form of questions:

1. What is the disciplinary status of sociology in India?
2. How far sociological concepts require further readaptation and reconceptualization for a scientific study of the Indian society?
3. What possibilities of interdisciplinary approach and cooperation are available and can be further envisaged?
4. What are the problems of teaching and research in sociology in India?
5. What further improvements can be brought about?
6. What is the role of sociology and sociologists in a developing society?
7. What theoretical and practical problems must be taken up for research by the sociologists in India?[37]

Some of the relevant conclusions are:

1. No prescriptive formulae for sociological enterprise could be laid down and the practice of sociology should be left to the academic sensibility of individual sociologists themselves.
2. There was no antinomy between the use of historical fact and the structural-functional approach.
3. The discussions also revealed the faith of sociologists in the universalistic character of sociology for India.
4. The possibility of a typical and particularistic sociology was rejected.[38]

The Department of Sociology was established at Delhi University in 1959, with M.N. Srinivas as its senior member of the faculty. Under Srinivas' stewardship, studies on caste, kinship, family and village community were carried out with theoretical and methodological orientation of the British social anthropology, particularly the one represented by Radcliffe-Brown. The group of scholars led by Srinivas was not represented in either Agra or Mount Abu seminars on sociology for/in India. The Marxist sociologists also were not represented in the two seminars. Saran, who wrote a paper on Indian sociology around the same time, writes: 'Marxist sociology has not developed in India in a systematic manner.'[39] Saran mentions B.N. Dutta's studies on Indian social polity as a Marxist interpretation of the caste system in which its origin is traced from the formation of economic classes. S.A. Dange's book – *India from Primitive Communism to Slavery*, and D.D. Kosambi's – *Understanding of the Ancient Indian History* are other examples noted by Saran.

Saran also classified the thinking in Indian sociology into: (a) those who totally rejected the modern Western civilization and advocated the return to the traditional principles; (b) those who wanted a synthesis of the two; and (c) those who debated the basis of synthesis – (i) traditional concepts and institutions in terms of modern rationalistic-positivistic ideas, and (ii) a value-neutral scientific attitude.[40] Saran considered Anand K. Coomaraswamy and Radhakamal Mukerjee as the representatives of two traditions, namely, the traditional theory of man and society, and a multidimensional and holistic analysis and outlook, respectively. Saran put up D.P. Mukerji with Radhakamal Mukerjee. The former was a critic of the latter.

The other points discussed by Saran are Indian social thought as sociology, community studies and sociology and social engineering.[41] Saran's essay on Indian sociology is an exercise in 'negation' of the existing theories and approaches. He does not point out his own view in this essay. However, Saran seems to be in somewhat conformity with Coomaraswamy's view of a traditional theory of society and man. Saran, as we know, does not accept Western theories to be relevant for studying Indian society. Saran rejects American and British sociological theories as well as Marxism.

It is evident that a great deal of awareness exists among the Indian sociologists about the growth of sociology as a discipline. They have taken up self-introspection by analysing origin of the discipline and levels of its growth. The influences of the Western sociology (both American and British) and Marxism have been taken up with a view to understand the constraints and challenges shown by the discipline. It is denied that the founding fathers of sociology, namely, Comte, Marx, Weber and Durkheim did not influence teaching and research in sociology in India. It has also been conclusively proved that sociology in India, particularly in the 19th century and the first half of the 20th century, was not simply an imitation of the Western theories, concepts and methods of research. It was contemporaneous to sociology in the West.

The debate in the 1950s and 1960s was: Whether sociology in India should have a universal character or it should be unique in nature due to the uniqueness of Indian society? This question was taken up in two seminars and in several papers published in books and journals. We find that Indian sociologists were divided on this issue. However, a majority of them felt that it should be a part of general sociological theory, and there should be a synthesis and reinforcement of the general with the 'specific'. However, when this debate was going on, Louis Dumont gave a boosting to the 'culturological' view about the study of Indian society. We shall take up this debate later on.

Theory, method and data are the most important elements of a discipline, in addition to epistemology and philosophy. We have referred to these elements in a general way in the debate on sociology in India. However, we will be able to discuss them when we analyse some selected studies of the Indian village and social stratification. Extreme views are found in Indian sociology, for example, one taken up by Radhakamal Mukerjee and the other by A.K. Saran. Again, Damle finds Parsons' structural-functionalism as the most appropriate framework for analysing Indian social system. A.R. Desai advocates the orthodox Marxist approach as most suitable for understanding Indian society and state. G.S. Ghurye, R.N. Saxena and A.K. Saran hold views different from each other, but they conform to what is known as a 'traditionalist' perspective. Srinivas and his associates have found British functionalism as the most suitable approach. Y. Singh, Indra Deva and some others adhere to a sort of positivistic-empirical orientation and suggest for a 'synthesis' of general and specific dimensions in regard to sociology in India.

Notes

1. Cf. Y. Singh, 'Scope and method of sociology in India', in T.K.N. Unnithan, et al. (eds) *Sociology for India,* New Delhi: Prentice-Hall of India (P) Ltd., 1967, pp. 13–37.
2. Ibid., p. 20.
3. Bela Dutt Gupta, *Sociology in India,* Calcutta (now Kolkata): Centre for Sociological Research, 1972, p. xi.
4. Ibid., pp. 12–13.
5. Ibid., p. 14.
6. Ibid., p. 17.
7. Ibid., p. 83.
8. See, Louis Dumont and D.F. Pocock, *Contributions to Indian Sociology,* Vol. I, 1957.
9. See, *Contributions to Indian Sociology* from 1957 to 1966 and there-after its New Series. We will discuss later on at length the debate on 'For a Sociology of India'.
10. A couple of articles have also appeared in *Sociological Bulletin* in the 1970s. We shall discuss them too in the next chapter.
11. See, *Sociology in India,* Seminar papers (10–20 December, 1965), Agra: Institute of Social Sciences, Agra University.
12. T.K.N. Unnithan, et al. (eds), *Sociology for India,* New Delhi: Prentice-Hall of India, 1967.
13. See, Y. Singh's two essays in T.K.N. Unnithan, et al. (eds), op. cit.
14. R.N. Saxena, 'Sociology in India', in *Sociology in India,* op. cit. (1965), pp. 1–13. The same essay has appeared in T.K.N. Unnithan et al. (eds), pp. 61–70.
15. L. Dumont and D.F. Pocock, op. cit., 1957.
16. R.N. Saxena, op. cit., 1965, p. 11.
17. Ibid., p. 12.
18. Indra Deva, 'Possibility of an Indian sociology', in *Sociology in India,* op. cit., 1965, p. 68.
19. See, Anand K. Coomaraswamy, *The Dance of Siva,* Bombay (now Mumbai): Asia Publishing House, 1948.
20. Indra Deva, op. cit., 1965. The same article has appeared in T.K.N. Unnithan, et al. (eds), op. cit., 1967, pp. 71–84.
21. Y.B. Damle, 'For a theory of Indian sociology', in *Sociology in India,* op. cit., 1965, pp. 32–53. Under the same heading, it has appeared in T.K.N. Unnithan et al. (eds), op. cit., 1967, pp. 85–103.

22. Ibid., 41.
23. Y.B. Damle, 'Reference group theory and mobility in the caste system', in James Silverberg (ed.), *Social Mobility in the Caste System in India,* The Hague: Mouton & Co., 1968.
24. Y.B. Damle, op. cit., 1965, pp. 47–48.
25. Y. Singh, op. cit., 1965, p. 55.
26. Ibid., p. 60.
27. Ibid., p. 61.
28. Ibid., p. 66.
29. Y. Singh, op. cit., 1967, p. 19.
30. Ibid., p. 20.
31. Ibid., p. 21.
32. Yogendra Singh, 'Academic role-structure and modernization: a study of university teachers' in S. Saberwal (ed.), *Beyond the Village: Sociological Explorations,* Simla: Indian Institute of Advanced Study, 1972, pp. 193–244.
33. Y. Singh, op. cit., 1967, p. 31.
34. Ibid., p. 32.
35. Ibid., p. 34.
36. Ibid., p. 37.
37. Y. Singh, 'Sociology for India: the emerging perspective', in T.K.N. Unnithan, et al. (eds), op. cit., 1967, p. 170.
38. Ibid., p. 171.
39. A.K. Saran, 'India', in Joseph S. Roucek (ed.), *Contemporary Sociology,* New York: Greenwood Press Publishers, 1958, p. 1013 (fn. 8).
40. Ibid., pp. 1013–1014.
41. Ibid., pp. 1023–1033.

CHAPTER 3

Sociology in India

A Sociology of Knowledge Perspective

We intend to discuss sociology in India from the point of its theory, methodology and data in this chapter. We shall limit our discussion mainly to the debate that has appeared in *Contributions to Indian Sociology*, including the one in the New Series, articles that have appeared in *Sociological Bulletin* and *Economic and Political Weekly*, and a couple of other articles and books that have come out on this theme. The emphasis in the debate is on: Whether sociology in India should concern itself with the study of values or it should study relations? The corollary of this question is: Whether the approach would be Indological (or culturological) or comparative? The main points of interest in a given study are: the method of study and the material to be studied. Now, the question is: Is Indology a historical science? Is Indological study diachronic in nature? How far a study of relations would do justice to diachrony? The question whether Indian society should be studied 'from within' or 'from without' or from both 'within and without' has also been taken up in view of the complexity, diversity, and unity of Indian society. This refers to what is known as 'home-made model' and 'external point of view'. In other words, it poses the problem of culturology vs positivism for studying Indian society. It is mentioned that D.P. Mukerji had 'positive-cum-subjective' approach by combining the view from within (study of tradition) and the view from without (Marxology). This point is related to the nature of Indian sociology in regard to its universal vs specific nature.

What is the nature of sociology in India? There cannot be a straight answer to this question. It is Hindu sociology – is one view; it is Indian sociology – is another view. It is Indological or culturological or it is universal (general) positivistic social science – is again a different view. It has the hangover of British colonialism and the academic hegemony of the West on the one hand, and the input of the 'Hindu chauvinism', and Indian nationalism, on the other.

How to arrange the material on the nature of Indian sociology from 1957 to 1982 (over a quarter-century) is really a problem before us. There is no order in the debate over these years. The same questions and points have been raised back and forth. We shall take up the debate the way it has grown, but our main points of discussion would revolve around theory, method and data. Our impression is that the debate has concentrated more on theory and method than data. There has been an effort to classify the literature on Indian sociology from a theoretical perspective right from 1965.[1] Recently, Ramkrishna Mukherjee[2] and R.S. Khare[3] have also provided classifications of sociologists engaged in researches on India. We shall analyse these classifications and other analytic schemes.

A Sociology of Values or a Value-Loaded Sociology

Dumont and Pocock, in the first article of the first number of *Contributions to Indian Sociology*, suggest their specific viewpoint 'for a sociology of India'.[4] They write: 'In our opinion, the first condition for a sound development of a sociology of India is found in the establishment of the proper relation between it and classical sociology. We wish to show how on one side the construction of an *Indian Sociology* (emphasis added) rests in part upon the existence of Indology, and how, on the other hand, far from its results being confined to its own domain, it can hope in its turn to widen and deepen the understanding of India, present and past, to which Indology is devoted.'[5] They further observe: 'In principle, a sociology of India lies at the point of confluence of Sociology and Indology.'[6] R.N. Saxena agrees with this Indological or scriptural basis of studying Indian society.[7] The basic premise of Dumont and Pocock is that 'India is one',[8] that 'the unity of India is a sort of common place'.[9] Castes are found throughout the country, and this speaks for India's *oneness.* They write in an assertive tone: 'Unity is found here above all *in ideas and values*'[10] (emphasis added). Unity is *social* in nature as *Indian society as a whole* could be seen by these ideas and values. Unity is found in terms of *relations* also (caste system is an evidence of this).

Dumont and Pocock accept the *relevance of* what they call *descriptive sociology* for India. Such a sociology is based on monographic field work by a trained anthropologist. However, this does not mean that an empirical group becomes a legitimate object of study. An empirical group or a segment of a caste or a village cannot be isolated from its milieu. Their view is that the primary principle of sociology forbids us to abstract a phenomenon from its social context.[11] In India, the relation between an empirical group and its environment is social in the strictest sense.[12] Thus, Dumont and Pocock do not approve the idea of conducting 'monographic or regional' studies, or studies confining to a state or a linguistic group, etc. Their view is that instead of highlighting regional or national diversities or differences, we should emphasize the common civilization or pan-Indian patterns.

In regard to 'descriptive sociology', they observe: 'to say description is to say understanding'.[13] This is true in three ways:

1. 'because there are no sociological facts unless and until we speak of them, i.e. we express the data in sociological language;
2. we do not claim to "explain isolated traits", but tend to count for each of them by the system of which it is a part; and
3. our primary object is a system of ideas.'[14]

They formulate their view on Indian sociology in terms of interpretations of Indological data as part of the entire system and its values. They further assert: 'It is a matter then, broadly speaking, of a sociology of values: first we must describe the common values and take care not to mix up facts of "representation" with facts of "behaviours"'.[15] 'We must learn from the people themselves which modes of thinking we have the right to apply and which we should reject'.[16]

Thus, the *value-load* in Dumont and Pocock's thesis is to take for granted that (a) India is one; (b) Indology is representative of people's behaviour or that it guides people's behaviour in a significant way; (c) unity in ideas and values is *social* in nature; (d) unity and differences cannot co-exist; and (e) people's mode of thinking and not their modes of actual relations should be taken as data. These points speak of Dumont and Pocock's value-load in sociology. Surprisingly, differences between North and South India, between literate and illiterate, between the rich and the poor, between the 'powerful' and the 'weak' do not matter to Dumont and Pocock as all of them are guided by the same principle known as the *caste system*. In our view, caste is not simply a system of ideas and values. It is more than a ritualistic system. Historians have convincingly proved that it has been a dynamic system; its corporateness has been challenged from time to time; mobility and migration have taken place due to caste conflicts. All these and other vital facts have been ignored by these architects of 'a sociology of values'.

Some other points related to Dumont and Pocock's 'for a sociology of India' are: (a) the notion of purity and impurity; (b) caste as a system of values; (c) India's basic unity in terms of its social organization; and (d) hierarchy – the encompassing and the encompassed or institutionalized inequality. Sociology in India for Dumont and Pocock cannot go beyond an analysis of socio-religious values of Hindus. It is difficult to find out the *real* purpose of their emphasis on Indology as a methodological tool and on 'values' as a frame of reference. These apriori constraints lead to serious distortions of Indian society, and their analysis amounts to 'reductionism'. What is 'ideal' is treated as 'real', and what is 'real' is neglected from the analysis. Let us, now look at F.G. Bailey's review of Dumont and Pocock's view in 'For a sociology of India'.[17]

F.G. Bailey's Critique of the Dumont-Pocock Approach

F.G. Bailey in a critique of Dumont and Pocock's 'For a sociology of India' observes that their style is 'infectious', perspective is too narrow, and they define 'sociology' out of existence. They have designed a 'straitjacket' for 'Indian sociology'. Bailey picks up a few points from Dumont and Pocok's essay related to their object of study, namely, *Indian Society as a whole.* Understanding is achieved by the abstraction of a system, the elements in this system are ideas as they state: 'our primary object is a system of ideas'. Ideas are 'the principles that the people themselves give', and behind these principles are 'necessary but implicit links.'[18] Bailey thinks that one should not confine his analysis to the raw material (people's principles), and one should not concern only with abstracting out consistent elements. Bailey puts his view lucidly as follows: 'A valid sociological understanding can be achieved, given certain problems, by making abstractions immediately from behaviour or from other non-verbal information, and by using only our own concepts and evading the ideas of the people (supposing they have any ideas, which is not always the case). In other words, sociology does not consist only of a sociology of values, and a part of our understanding can be derived from behaviour. This is not to deny that there is a sociology of values, but only to say that "what it is that people believe and think" is not the whole field of sociology, as the editors seem to me arguing'.[19] The editors feel that they have been misunderstood by Bailey. In a textual note, they write: 'In our view, it can be argued that we make too much of ideas or that we put them unduly at the beginning, but not that we are exclusively after a "sociology of values".'[20]

Bailey's emphasis is on the understanding of 'structural facts', which is quite evident in his book – *Caste and the Economic Frontier*.[21] Analysis of Indian society as a system of values or ideas becomes a strait-jacket, in which only a limited range of social phenomena can be fitted into. The ideas of 'unity', 'complexity', and 'people's principles' automatically do not make 'a sociology of values'. To treat Aryans and Dravidians, tribes and castes, caste and village at par, would amount to utter ignorance of the 'complexity' of Indian society and denial of its historical ramifications. These are considered as 'distortions' by Bailey.[22] Tribe and village exist as sociological realities independent of the caste system. Bailey observes: 'One wonders also whether the editors would agree that those villages which are "isolated" have "sociological reality".'[23]

Dumont and Pocock do not explain why they have preferred Indology or culturology 'for a sociology of India'. Is it not an attempt towards academic indoctrination of scholars interested in the study of Indian society? Is it that they think for the welfare of Indian sociology by bringing ideas which would reinforce and relegitimize India's caste system? While commenting on Iravati Karve's book – *Kinship Organisation in India*,[24] they suggest that Karve should choose between sociology and culturology. Bailey observes that 'this taunt could well be directed at themselves'.[25] Iravati Karve's work on kinship provides a wholesome analysis of the subject by combining Indology and field work, unity and diversity, ideas and practices. It is a good example of anthropological phenomenology.

Bailey says that Dumont and Pocock talk of 'Indian sociology', but they do not talk of 'Indian chemistry'. They do not make a rigorous distinction between cultural and social facts. Their definition of cultural facts (values, ideas or caste) rules out *comparison* of India with other societies and within India with different components and segments. Thus, Bailey is not for a particularistic sociology. Bailey writes: 'The uniqueness is *scientifically* incomprehensible. The unique can be comprehended only intuitively or through a mystical experience. I forebear to suggest that the editors have had this experience although their style suggests it.'[26]

Bailey quotes Nadel that 'society' is a higher level of abstraction than is culture.[27] This is also accepted by Y. Singh in his analysis of *Modernization of Indian Tradition*.[28] Bailey is quite forthright in his criticism of Dumont and Pocock's view and in advancing his own view about understanding of Indian society. He writes: 'In my view a knowledge of cultural values is only the beginning or the raw material of sociological analysis.'[29] Bailey's view is that one should make a sociological analysis of culture as one does of language, religion, etc. He feels that 'what the editors are advocating is not sociology at all, but a form of culturology'.[30] Only culturology can be made distinctively Indian. The editors use the phrase 'science of sociology,' but it seems that they have used it for 'knowledge'.[31] The other point is that how 'science of sociology' could become 'Indian' sociology, as a science deals in *systems*.[32] Bailey states: 'There can be no "Indian" sociology except in a "vague geographic sense", any more than there are distinctively Indian principles in chemistry or biology.'[33]

Finally, Bailey calls the editors view as a 'very odd kind of inverted ethnocentrism'.[34] The editors have not clearly expressed their view; their view is more of an assertion than evidence; and they have used an emotive language.[35] The editors express that Indian sociology is a branch of culturology. 'In fact, sociology in India is a part of sociology elsewhere.'[36] The editors' view that 'real structural changes' are a rare phenomenon, is also not acceptable to Bailey.[37]

Other Critiques of Dumont's Approach and Dumont's Reply

Dumont and Pocock reply Bailey's criticisms of their 'For a sociology of India'.[38] Dumont also responds to A.K. Saran's review of Dumont and Pocock's position regarding Indian sociology,[39] and Dumont also gives his view on T.N. Madan's defence[40] of Dumont and Pocock in – 'A Fundamental Problem in the Sociology of Caste'.[41] Let us, take up some other important points of this debate, that runs from 1957 to 1966. We have already discussed the main points of Dumont and Pocock's culturology and Bailey's structural analysis in this connection.

In their rejoinder to Bailey,[42] the editors make it clear that sociology is a special kind of science and the sociologist looks at his data from without and from within.[43] Madan does not agree with Dumont and Pocock regarding the external point of view, which, they say that the sociologist shares with the natural scientist.[44] Saran also expressed a similar view before Madan. Saran writes: 'Social reality qua reality has no "outside" ... the only outside is its interpretation in terms of an alien culture ... .'[45] Madan accepts that there is a view from within the society studied, and here he agrees with Saran, but he is doubtful of the 'external point of view', which the editors share with the natural scientist.[46] Dumont admits a 'combine' of the two viewpoints. However, he does not agree either with Saran's or with Madan's criticism of their (Dumont and Pocock's) position.[47]

Madan makes two points: (a) that by taking an internal view one surrenders a 'truly external position', and (b) so far Dumont-Pocock maintain the external view, their position is not opposed to that of Bailey.[48] Thus, according to Madan, both Dumont-Pocock and Bailey's views may be subsumed under positivism. But Dumont raises questions about Madan's view. Dumont's view is that positivism exclusively refers to the 'external view', and this is not applicable to Dumont and Pocock as they take a serious cognizance of Indology. However, Dumont feels that the external view can be combined with the internal view, and their position may be treated as *positive-cum-subjective.* This is another modification we note in the Dumont-Pocock position of 1957 by Dumont in 1966. Earlier, we have referred to the modification that the editors are not exclusively after a 'sociology of values'. Dumont admits that they should have used the expression 'sociology of India', instead of 'Indian sociology'. They also admit that they were not aware of the fact that there was a periodical, *The Indian Sociologist* in the early part of the 20th century. It is regretted that they knew of B.K. Sarkar's *Hindu Sociology* only.[49]

Saran considers the combining of the internal and external views as *positivistic hybris.* Saran thinks that the interpretation of one culture in terms of another is simply meaningless, or ontologically nil. Different cultures cannot be compared. Man is an ontologically non-being abstraction. The one who looks from outside imposes perspective of his culture in understanding the other society. Saran writes: '... taking, in the name of science, modernity or objectivity, is a firmly provincial standpoint for the study of traditional or tradition-haunted societies.'[50] I. Ahmad observes that studies on Hindus and their tradition are more than other communities. Indian nationalism is expressed in Hindu idiom. Indian sociology could be called a Hindu sociology.[51] However, this view is not quite true factually, and its logical conclusions are quite nasty in nature.

Dumont refers to Saran's view as 'cultural solipsism'. Dumont observes that 'duality' is necessarily part of anthropological or sociological research. 'External view', comparison and objectivity are necessary parts of a 'proper' understanding of Indian society. Dumont's view is that if the Western sociology had scientific temper and applied to Indian society as well, construction of Indian sociology independent of that would have been a wrong attempt.[52] 'A Hindu sociology is a contradiction in terms ...' Dumont disregards the role of sociocentrism in sociology. 'Sociology is one in its principle.'[53] Particularly, reacting to Saran's observations, Dumont writes: 'What is actually found under its label may be good or bad, scientific or not, understanding or not; there may be found within it different tendencies; but there never will be two sociologies, let alone a sociology of solipsism.'[54]

India can contribute to universal sociology both directly and indirectly. Global features of Indian society should be translated into sociological language. The Indian type of hierarchy, Dumont finds, is a universal tool for a better understanding of the modern Western society itself.[55] Sociology reflects the social experience of mankind. Reacting to Saran, Dumont writes: 'Progressive Indians should be particularly alert against the danger of fake or "Hindu" sociology developing as a weapon of obscurantism and reaction.'[56] Madan broadly agrees with Saran and responds to his criticism by Dumont.[57]

Apparently, Dumont, Saran and Saxena might appear different from each other in regard to their perspectives about Indian sociology, but the result of their analyses has been the same. Dumont may talk of 'the external view' or 'positivist-cum-subjective' view, he ultimately praises *caste system* and its sanctions related to institutionalized inequality through the concept of *hierarchy*. He seeks approval of his view from Mauss and Hocart.[58] The first refers to the force of 'social', which is 'caste' in India, the latter writes about the ritualistic theory of caste. Hutton talks of functions of caste,[59] thereby meaning it as a beneficial institution. Not only Hutton, other British administrators-cum-ethnographers have also given an optimistic picture of caste and other institutions.[60] Perhaps, this was the demand of the British Raj in India. The Western scholars have defined caste and class as antithetical institutions, and at the same time they have praised Western society and class, and have defined caste as an archaic and oriental institution, working against democratic ethos. But, at the same time, they have praised caste as a useful institution for Indian society.

Why such contradictory and biassed views and definitions have been given by these Western scholars is a question which should be taken up seriously and sincerely. Dumont can blame Saran for wrong 'hypothetical-deductive reasoning', for 'irrelevant quotations', and for his 'neo-Hindu creed',[61] but why Dumont gives such an enormous premium to culturology and caste system and its allied institutions remains a sort of mysticism. Why Indian caste system becomes a datum for Dumont to develop a global sociology? Dumont's absolutist view has its history in the one-sided study of Indian society. One concrete result of such a view is that differences, conflicts, interests, exploitations, and uneven access to resources and opportunities have not become as relevant phenomena for sociological understanding. A study of these aspects would have provided an understanding for giving a challenge to the colonizers. Today, it could give a challenge to the Western sociology if caste was not studied on the line suggested by Hutton, Hocart, Dumont, etc. Dumont's polemics would not strengthen his view on Indian society. The question is: What approach is relevant for studying Indian society? Should the approach be Radcliffe-Brownian or Dumontian or Levi-Straussian or Marxian? It cannot be an approach based on scriptures or ancient texts. The question is not that 'ideas' are more important or 'relations' are more important from a methodological point of view. It is a question of having a real understanding of Indian society, its social formation, particularly of its contemporaneity to understand the present with clarity and reliability. Such an exercise has not so far been a part of the sociologist's infrastructure and understanding.

Some More Points in the Debate for a Sociology of India

The debate on 'For a Sociology of India' takes a different form after Dumont and Pocock stopped editing the *Contributions to Indian Sociology*. In fact, Dumont withdrew from it as he writes in 'A Farewell'[62] to Contributions to Indian Sociology. Let us once again state that the Marxist and the neo-Marxist sociologists still did not join the debate in Contributions, and debate also did not remain as 'alive' as it was up to 1966. A couple of short articles have appeared and we shall give a brief resume of the post-1966 debate.

J.P.S. Uberoi looks at the aim and method of science as uniform and universal, but the problem of science is seen in relation to a given society. As such, Uberoi writes: 'The sociology of knowledge is a study of urgent practical importance today, for some consideration of it should form the prolegomenon and background to the determination of particular priorities and objectives.'[63] Advancement of science cannot be separated from the advancement of independence in India. According to Uberoi, false cosmopolitanism and false humanitarianism must go.

Srinivas prefers the concept of Westernization in place of modernization because the former entails the values of humanitarianism and egalitarianism.[64] It is really an irony of our scholars that they have found human values in colonization of the Indian masses. Uberoi rightly observes that 'as a social institution science, national or international, cannot and does not live outside its era:'[65] '... Scientistic internationalism is a bridge of illusion, a cloak of comfort across the chasm.'[66]

Y. Singh takes a position[67] comparable with R.K. Merton's view[68] about nature of sociological theory. According to Singh, sociological theory in India does not have a 'formal' status of theory. Theory is rare, but approaches are far too many. There are typologies and classifications. Singh questions: 'Do we find a paradigm reflecting theoretic simplicity and power in Dumont's formulation of Indian sociology?' The other question is: 'Is the definitional range of his primitive concepts such that his sociology is able to (a) translate sociological data interculturally, and (b) deal with all the significant range of societal and cultural facts which are relevant to Indian sociology?'[69] Y. Singh's answer is 'no' to these questions. He does not accept Dumont's idea of 'functionally equivalent concepts.' 'Sociology of development'[70] and 'change' does not matter for Dumont. Singh states that 'Dumont is more concerned with system integration and maintenance than with change or conflict'.[71] For Singh, sociology means a system of operational concepts and societal self-consciousness. 'Sociology is a science and its theoretic structure should not differ basically from natural sciences.'[72] According to Singh, the search for a sociology of India may not logically contradict the general and scientific nature of sociology.[73]

D. Narain is of the view that questions raised by Dumont-Pocock are not urgent and of a general nature as they refer to the relationship between history and sociology or between culture and society.[74] A number of important questions are raised by Narain. These are as follows:

1. Is the diachronic-synchronic polarity an analytical distinction or does this distinction really inhere in social reality?
2. Is a wholly synchronic study possible?

3. Does it not imply freezing time which is clearly out of question?
4. If the wholly synchronic approach is not possible, what is the controversy about?
5. Is a study historical if it spans centuries and not if it spans only decade(s)?

There are some more questions raised by Narain:

1. Must one always go to the very beginning of a thing in order to fully understand its contemporary form and function(s)?
2. Are there no strategic moments in time which can be used as convenient starting points?
3. Is the whole past undifferentiated into periods, equally valid for the understanding of everything in contemporary society?
4. Must we always go to the ancient sources to understand everything in Indian society of today?[75]

Narain deals with both disciplinary and methodological questions. He is certainly not for diachrony at the cost of synchrony. He does not surrender sociology to history for generalization. He writes: 'By removing the absolute distinction between the diachronic and synchronic approaches, one also removes the need to surrender sociology to history. Good history is as much dependent on sociology as good sociology is dependent upon history.'[76] Narain is not for 'unique'. 'Concentration on the unique, inevitably tending to exclude, or at least reduce comparison and generalization, will surely limit knowledge and understanding.'[77]

Distinction between insider and outsider is not quite relevant for Narain as he observes that 'the fact of the matter is that a rank outsider has no way of feeling interested in a phenomenon to which he is a *total* outsider.'[78] An alliance between scientific and humanistic approaches can be brought out without saying that one is more powerful than the other. In nutshell, Narain is for a scientific approach which basically emphasizes study of the present, and if necessary, the relevant past is taken into account.

Madan summarizes the debate in *Contributions to Indian Sociology*,[79] and again agrees with Dumont's position about Indian sociology. However, Madan is unfair to a few important sociologists who have provided schema of studies on Indian society. Y. Singh's *Modernization of Indian Tradition*,[80] and his articles on Indian sociology have been ignored. Ramkrishna Mukherjee's earlier books and articles[81] and the book on Indian sociology have also been left out. One gets the impression from Madan's view as if 'positivism' and 'culturology' alone have influenced and shaped sociology in India. Variants of Marxism and structural-functionalism and structuralist perspectives have been debated and tested by several scholars, but remain ignored on Madan's analysis.

Towards Theory and Methodology of Indian Sociology

We shall discuss the main points of theorization in Indian sociology within the specific context and milieu of Indian society. The immediate context is that India had colonial cognitive traditions in the past, and it has become an independent nation since 1947, and this provides it a new context and milieu. A sociology of knowledge perspective would demand examination of the continuity/discontinuity of the colonial/traditional approaches, concepts and methods of study. The units and themes of study are not independent of their context and milieu.

Y. Singh observes that even the debate whether sociology has universal concepts and techniques or it refers to culturally oriented cognitive styles and structures could be seen in the context of the hangover of colonialism in independent India.[82] Today, the tensions in Indian sociology are between (a) the 'Master theory' or 'General theory' and 'conceptual schemes', and (b) between 'universalism' of concepts and propositions and their 'particularism' or 'contextuality'. The third source of tension is the role of ideology in theory construction.[83]

Let us, take up some more points of this important essay on ideology, theory and methods in Indian sociology by Singh, which covers a period of a quarter-century of sociology in India from 1952 to 1977. However, we have made use of literature on Indian sociology up to 1982. Singh divides this period into four parts:

1. *1952 to 1960*: A period of adaptive changes and innovations;
2. *1960 to 1965*: A period of significant shifts in theoretic priorities and the beginning of some critical tensions in theory and ideology of Indian sociology;

3. *1965 to 1970*. A period of marked sociological self- awareness and growth of new directions in theoretical and substantive contributions; and
4. *1970 to 1977*: A period of new maturity and exploring both theoretically and substantively new horizons of knowledge.

These four periods correspond with four theoretic developments in Indian sociology. These theoretic orientations are: (a) philosophical, (b) culturological, (c) structural, and (d) dialectical-historical. Singh states that Indian sociologists have been less concerned with constructing meta-theories or general theories, and they have been more prone to using conceptual schema for analysis of social problems.[84] Somewhat differently, this point has also been made by Madan while reacting on Dumont-Pocock's view on sociology of India.[85] Any way, Singh observes that the only exception is Radhakamal Mukerjee who proposes a *general integrated social sciences model for explanation and understanding of social realities* in *The Philosophy of Social Sciences*.[86] Singh states that some Marxist scholars, particularly A.R. Desai,[87] have used a general theory but have analysed substantive realities from an ideological position rather than on the relative power of theoretical systems.[88]

The works of Radhakamal Mukerjee, D.P Mukerji and A.K. Saran[89] are included in the philosophical orientation. Singh provides a detailed comparative analysis of these three different orientations on a continuum. Dumont, Srinivas, Singer and Marriott[90] are the chief representatives of the culturological approach. The structural theoretic orientation in Indian sociology refers to the writings of Bailey, Beteille, Aggarwal, Arora, Bhatt, Brass, D'Souza, Joshi, R. Singh, P.N. Mukherji, IP. Desai, M.S.A. Rao, and a host of several other sociologists[91]; who have been working on social stratification, agrarian structures, social movements, kinship and family and disputes, etc. The studies by D.P. Mukerji, Ramkrishna Mukherjee, A.R. Desai, Charles Bettelheim and by some economists and historians[92] could be included under the dialectical-historical orientation.

Ideology, culture or tradition, structure and dialectics are the key concerns of these four theoretic orientations, respectively. There are a few points which one could take up for investigation.

(a) The periods do not synchronize with the dominance or prominence of these approaches. The tendency of going back and forth is found in regard to these orientations. (b) It is assumed that the sociologists[93] took up mainly those problems for investigation which were of crucial significance and urgency for the people. The question whether the 'scientism' and fashions of the discipline guided the selection of research problems or the research was demanded by society for gaining understanding of its problems, has been left undecided by Y. Singh. Singh inclines to have more concern for 'systematics of sociology' with a 'positivistic' bias rather than for ontologically determined concepts and categories. His love for systematization and classificatory skill could be seen in his writings from 1965 onwards.[94] However, he gives premium to the interaction between the general theories and culture-specific data. This is evidenced in Singh's book *Modernization of Indian Tradition*[95] and in the 'trend reports' for ICSSR on social stratification[96] and social change[97] in India.

A somewhat different perspective is advanced by Singh in an earlier essay.[98] An assumed international 'reference model' of social science and the slow pace of Indian social transformation itself have conditioned the character and evaluation of Indian social sciences in general, and sociology and social anthropology in particular. Singh examines sociology in India from the perspective of the sociology of knowledge. He writes: 'The relationship between the conceptual and methodological baggage of the Western social science and its relevance to an understanding of the historico-specific problems of various societies lies in the domain of the sociology of knowledge.'[99] How the Western theoretic constructs, methodologies and techniques of research have been accepted by Indian sociology and to what extent they have gone well with historical specificities of Indian society is the most relevant question to be examined from the point of sociology of knowledge. A few questions are referred by Y. Singh in the essay under discussion:

1. 'What is the logical or substantive relevance of social science paradigms developed in a different historical context for another country which is historically and existentially different'?[100]

2. 'How far have social sciences responded to the various phases of social-structural transformation in India and the corresponding needs of a world-view and sociocultural identity of their own society'?[101]
3. 'How far have the existential conditions in India influenced their growth'?[102]

A few statements may be picked up in the form of answers to the above questions. Historically, the building blocks, both of social anthropology and sociology in India, are derived from the Western colonialist interpretations of the Indian society. In its early phase, sociology had a deep imprint of the earlier colonial and ethnographic and social interpretative writings. 'Caste' was treated independent of 'tribe' and vice versa; and the Indian village was looked at as an isolated whole.[103] This was perhaps done for *promoting colonial power in India* (emphasis added). Thus, the basic issues related to feudalism, agrarian structure, reforms and movements remained untouched to a large extent.

Like Madan,[104] Singh also observes: 'Imitative social science tradition in India was a logical result of this fragmentation of sociological apperception.'[105] G.S. Ghurye, Radhakamal Mukerjee and D.P. Mukerji realised the imposition of Western social science and reacted to this by providing their own explanations for studying Indian society. Singh asks: 'Did this major historical change (India's independence) influence the social science paradigms in India?' 'Did social science mobilize itself to tackle the crucial issues of national consolidation and identity?'[106] Singh's answer to these is in the negative.

Our view is that undoubtedly there are two co-existent traditions in Indian sociology: (a) the colonialist, and (b) the imperialist. The 'nativist' tradition has not emerged as a challange to the forceful 'combine' of these two traditions. However, the debate has started questioning the role and relevance of the continuity of colonial elements and the hegemony of the Western social sciences' paradigms in the understanding of Indian society.

Finally, Singh raises the question: 'What should be the role of social science and social scientists in contemporary India?'[107] He writes: 'My argument is not that we should give up the scientific spirit in social science researches and substitute ideology for it.... I affirm that the task of science is to offer explanations of social phenomena in terms of prediction of causal relationships among various events. This should also hold good for the social sciences. The universalism of social science, however, in my opinion ends at this point of formal structure and methodology. Beyond this, the nature of social science is governed by the historicity of societal conditions .... My argument is that whatever may be the sophistications achieved by a particular research endeavour, its problem-selection and formulation of hypotheses is basically conditioned by the value-preferences of the researcher.'[108] Researcher becomes a 'variable' in terms of particular existential conditions, and this refers to the sociology of knowledge perspective.

Singh cautions us against the international or Western social science 'reference model' and its inherent concepts, tools and techniques, in other words, against 'methodological individualism' and social system ideology, and suggests greater use of history in sociological understanding.[109] Singh's this essay no doubt emphasizes the need for 'indigenization' of sociological understanding, but Singh is not prepared to bid a 'farewell' to the 'formal structure' and methodology of social science. The assumption that there is 'universalism of social science' is quite untenable. This 'universalism' could be called as 'particularism' of the British or American social science. Thus, Singh gives us cautious hints about the use of Western social science paradigms and concepts, but this exposition is only a slightly different view from his earlier position.[110]

A couple of articles provide narrative accounts of the history of sociology or teaching of sociology in Indian universities and colleges.[111] We shall discuss the two modes of thinking, which have emerged in Indian sociology in the 1970s. The one has a swing towards the Marxian approach and the other is the non-Marxian way of sociological understanding. A few selected representatives of the two categories could be taken up to illustrate this point.

The Marxist and the Non-Marxist Dispositions in Indian Sociology

Ramkrishna Mukherjee shows a strong Marxist disposition in his book – *The Rise and Fall of the East India Company*,[112] but in his other book – *Dynamics of a Rural Society*,[113] a modification of this disposition is evident as he uses 'interactional' relations between various classes as the device, by which the details of each class could be known to understand their differentiation. However, Mukherjee takes more of a methodological position than a Marxist or a modified Marxist view for studying Indian society in an article – 'Study of Social Change and Social Development in the Developing Societies'.[114] We shall refer this view of Mukherjee as his analysis combines both 'theory' and 'method' of study. Mukherjee claims his perspective to be both 'contemporary' and 'diagnostic'. He rejects the idea of a simple sequential model of social change. For Mukherjee, 'developing societies' are not unique. He writes: 'Universality in the development of sociology, therefore, will not be attained by a contextual and imitative application of any theory on these societies. Instead, empirical research on the mechanics of these societies (viz. *what, how,* and *why* of their statics and dynamics) will lead us to this goal.'[115]

Mukherjee brings home this point by saying that the current theories can be used for formulating hypotheses for studying 'developing societies' in terms of their *place, time* and *object* dimensions. He refers to the use of the Marxian and the Weberian concepts of social dynamics. Mukherjee writes: 'In order to draw objective and unambiguous generalizations from this approach, we require a commonly agreed frame of reference which locates a set of hierarchically structured units of observation, analysis and inference.'[116] 'Indicators' of the problem under investigation may be formulated *deductively* in terms of the *null hypotheses* (referring to no change) and the *alternate hypotheses* (referring to a time-series). A *research design* is required based on the concepts of statistical probability and multivariate analysis.[117] This leads to the research to collection of both quantitative and qualitative data-inductive investigation.

Mukherjee has a deep-seated desire to have a 'universality of science', by seeing its objective comprehensive particular manifestations. We would say that Mukherjee's approach suffers from a couple of limitations: (a) His deductive-inductive inferential approach becomes a straitjacket, and it emphasizes too much of methodologism, and theoretical apriorism becomes inevitable;

(b) existential determinism goes in the background and methodological nomology predominates; (c) a synthesis of value (frame of reference) and fact (actual research), diachrony and synchrony, structure and process, and quantitative and qualitative data is aimed at (as claimed by Mukherjee), but is not realized; and finally (d) the approach has not been put so far in practice, perhaps mainly due to its cumbersomeness.

In two subsequent articles,[118] Ramkrishna Mukherjee reinforces the view he develops about the study of social change and development in 'developing societies'. According to Mukherjee, four fundamental questions have to be answered in regard to the phenomena which a scientific discipline deals with: *what it is, how is it, why is it,* and *what will it be.* 'What' and 'how' refer to the understanding of social phenomena as entities or units, hence *descriptive stage* in social research. 'Why' refers to *explanatory stage,* and 'what will it be' refers to the *diagnostic stage.* The last stage follows from the first three questions and on the basis of probability denotes the structure, function and process of the contemporary phenomena in a dynamic perspective.[119] On this basis, Mukherjee distinguishes the following three stages in the historical development of Indian sociology:

1. Proto-professional stage of sociology prior to the twentieth century.
2. Professional stage of descriptive and explanatory sociology in the first half of the 20th century.
3. Currently needed stage of diagnostic sociology.[120]

The Indian sociology has reached at that critical point which demands diagnostic research and this would also enhance both *descriptions* and *explanation.* Mukherjee writes: 'In any scientific discipline an explanation may be: (a) relevant or irrelevant, if it is fallacious; (b) necessary or unnecessary, if it is *sui generis* to the given facts; (c) efficient or inefficient, if it is equivocal; and (d) sufficient or insufficient, if it is not comprehensive. The possibilities from these four sets of characteristics are as follows:

1. An explanation may not be relevant and therefore, not necessary, efficient and sufficient.

2. An explanation may be relevant but not necessary and therefore, not efficient and sufficient.
3. An explanation may be relevant and necessary but not efficient, and therefore, not sufficient.
4. An explanation may be relevant, necessary and efficient, but not sufficient.
5. An explanation may be relevant, necessary and efficient, but the demand of the discipline may be beyond explanation.'[121]

Though Ramkrishna Mukherjee suggests a blueprint of *diagnostic sociology* with a view to make sociology as a 'relevant' discipline for understanding India's multifarious problems, yet he is not able to spell out a clear line of thinking. Often he seeks support from speeches and writings of D.P. Mukerji, but D.P. Mukerji's combination of 'tradition' and 'Marxology' is not the source of Ramkrishna Mukherjee's (R.K.M.) strength. He draws more from positivistically-oriented 'logical and statistical' social sciences for understanding of Indian society.

Role of 'ideology' and deductive-positivistic orientation is again examined by R.K.M. in another essay – 'The Sociologist and the Social Reality',[122] by having a dialectical appreciation of a problem with an *inductive-inferential orientation*. Mukherjee writes: 'The problem before us is not that sociology contains value-loads, but how we may objectively treat the differential value-loads for an ever more precise, comprehensive, and unequivocal appraisal of the social reality.' 'An inductive- inferential approach is "value-free" and it examines the "value-loaded" images about reality and of the researcher'.[123] R.K.M. does not plead for an 'Indian science of sociology', nor D.P. Mukerji did by studying Indian traditions.[124] Myrdal's study of the countries of Asia,[125] with a common framework, gives an impression of developing an *Asian Sociology*, but R.K.M. does not approve of this too. He says that he has been labelled a 'bourgeois-Marxist' or a 'Marxist bourgeois', or merely a dilettante or purist, but he claims that he examines the role of ideology in understanding of social phenomena for achieving the status of a *diagnostic* discipline for sociology.[126] Finally, R.K.M. feels that the themes of research when diagnostically formulated would represent the issues of 'universal' appeal precisely and systematically, and this would also enhance causality and knowledge about social reality.

P.C. Joshi in his rambling 'reflections' on social science research in India[127] highlights the need for 'institutionalization of scientific activity' in independent India. Like R.K.M., a need for relating the 'general' features of science with 'specific' situation is emphasized by Joshi. However, Joshi does not offer a 'deductive-inductive-inferential' approach for social research as suggested by R.K.M. Joshi stresses on rejection of Western social science models and concepts, and insists on emergence of an 'involved' social scientist in India. But the perspective is not quite clear. He speaks of Myrdal's work as 'an immortal contribution to social science'.[128] A.R. Desai's work[129] has not been praised and only a passing reference is made that it has been unduly criticised by L. Dumont.[130] He talks of a 'scientific ethos', and seeks support for this idea from S. Andreski's book – *Social Sciences as Sorcery*,[131] which is full of polemics and negativism. Finally, Joshi claims to go along with D.P. Mukerji's approach, but he does not work on a sort of 'synthesis' of Indian tradition and Marxology. Eclecticism is pronounced in Joshi's treatment of the subject. For example, he makes a reference of Radhakamal Mukerjee, D.P. Mukerji and N.K. Bose's contributions to Indian sociology, but affords to forget G.S. Ghurye's contributions to Indian sociology and his catholicity in guiding his students in regard to their researches.

Prescriptions in sociology are abundantly available, particularly suggesting renovation of concepts, formulation and reformulation of hypotheses and application of new techniques of research. One of the suggestions is that Western social science could be used wherever it is found useful; another is that Marxist approach should be applied in a suitably modified fashion; and third suggestion is that a structural-historical perspective should be adopted in place of culturological analysis of Indian society. Self-critical appraisal[132] is another advice extended to the Indian sociologist. Gouldner and Andreski are ready references being suggested for conducting sociological research in India.

A.R. Desai applies the Marxist approach to the study of 'nationalism' in India during the British rule.[133] He spells out historical-dialectical materialism and applies it to the study of various types of movements, rural-urban relations, caste and class structure, social mobility, education and some other aspects.

Though Desai's book on nationalism was published in 1948, but it became more popular in the late 1960s and 1970s perhaps due to increased consciousness of Indian social scientists toward societal self-consciousness. In 1950s and early 1960s American structural-functionalism and British functionalism dominated social sciences in general and sociological research, in particular. However, Desai, undeterred by these imperialistic influences, continued to write on Indian society and state from the perspective of an involved Marxist scholarship.[134]

In his Presidential Address to the fifteenth All-India Sociological Conference, A.R. Desai narrates about twenty-seven points referring to the assessment of Indian sociology.[135] Desai finds that the dominant sociological approaches in India are basically non-Marxist, and the Marxist approach has been rejected on the pretext of its being dogmatic, value-loaded and deterministic in nature. The non-Marxist approaches are phenomenological, ethnomethodological, culturological, etc.[136] The relevant approach, according to Desai, is the Marxist approach, as it could help study of governmental policies, the classes entrenched into State apparatus and India's political economy. Desai writes: 'I wish the social science practitioners in India break through the atmosphere of allergy towards this profound and influential approach and create climate to study the growing body of literature articulating various aspects of Marxist paradigm.' Marxist approach emphasizes the study of *property relations* to understand Indian society, the class character of the state and the path of development.[137]

L. Dumont, while commenting on Desai's book – *Social Background of Indian Nationalism*[138], writes: 'More than University thesis, it is an overgrown political pamphlet clad in a university gown.'[139] Dumont makes a scathing and unsparing attack on Desai's approach. In fact, Dumont hates not only a Marxist approach but also any other non-Marxist approach except his own. Dumont's approach to Indian society represents rank conservative ideology and it also smells of the self-proclaimed superiority of the Western scholarship and Western society.

Now, let us look at some other observations on Indian sociology. Y. Singh's book *Modernization of Indian Tradition*[140] brought out a fundamental shift in theorization about Indian society by an Indian sociologist. It is a very well documented and systematic study of social change in independent India. It has been taken seriously by scholars of both Marxist and non-Marxist hues. H.C. Srivastava[141] rates it as a significant landmark in Indian sociology. But S. Chopra considers it a sort of 'establishment' or 'official' sociology.[142] Ramkrishna Mukherjee looks at the analysis of social change in India by Singh with a suspicion.[143] Analysis of interaction between religion and society in India's socio-historical context by K.P. Gupta is undertaken from a sociology of knowledge perspective.[144] Gupta recapitulates sociology of Hinduism. Saran is aware of 'what is "Indian" or "Modern" in India's modernity.'[145] Gupta, siding with Saran, writes: 'India's modernity is Indian but not modern because it is still rooted in the Hindu tradition.'[146] Further, 'India's modernity is modern but not Indian because it is consciously seeking to imitate the modernized west.'[147] This has led to a 'synthesis ideology' in India. In this synthesis, 'rational' Hindus are supposed to be living in a westernized Indian society. In Indian sociology, this ideology has prospered by accepting the Weberian framework. Weber provided to Indian sociologists a typical Hindu framework for viewing and explaining social change in terms of inner thought process, rather than institutional reform.[148]

Gupta considers Sarkar's *Hindu Sociology*, Srinivas' *Sanskritization* and Singh's *Modernization of Indian Tradition* as variations on the above theme. These sociologists draw a line between the Hindu religion and Hindu society, and the former remains intact, and the latter changes. Thus, 'modernity' is dissociated from religion. Gupta is unfair in clubbing Singh's thesis with Sarkar's Hinduistic and Srinivas' culturalistic understanding of Indian society. One finds in Singh's model of social change a semblance of orthogenetic and heterogenetic sources of change, levels of change, namely, primary and secondary, and structures in which change takes place, namely macro and micro. Thus, Singh's treatment of social change combines theory and empiricism and structure and culture.

A fuctionalist's perspective of sociology as a profession and sociologists as a professional community is given by D.A. Chekki.[149] Chekki analyses their academic background, fields of interest, membership of professional organization and nature of publications, etc. Momin examines the issue of 'identity' for Indian sociology. He writes: 'Indian sociology should have an active, humanistic and critical stance towards its subject-matter, but it should not get bogged down by revivalism and obscurantism.'[150] Indra Deva suggests use of folk and oral literature as data for sociological understanding. 'Social-Anthropological approach' is considered by Deva as most suitable for studying Indian society.[151]

In a long essay, R.S. Khare discusses the problem of 'external' vs 'internal' view about sociology of India.[152] He raises certain questions about the debate 'for a sociology of India', and notes that sociology is seeking 'nationalist identity', 'outside' debate is seen as a major theoretical and methodological issue in Indian sociology.[153] The main dimensions of the debate are: (a) the insider's view from 'inside', (b) the outsider's view from 'inside', (c) the outsider's view from 'outside', and (d) the insider's view from 'outside'. These positions are represented by Saran, Dumont, Bailey and Srinivas, respectively.[154] This debate (on Indian sociology) has become a 'manageric' of diverse issues – as between indigenous and analytic models, positive science and historiography, 'inside' view and 'outside' view, duality of form and content, particularization and generalization, the conscious and the unconscious, and predominant ideology and the 'fact'.[155] A few more dimensions have been added such as 'Science and Swaraj', patterns of dominance and dependence, nationalism vs internationalism, synchronic and diachronic approaches, and the Hindu and the non-Hindu dimensions of 'the Indian' social sciences in general, and of sociology in particular.[156] Inside-outside dichotomy is clearly evident in Indian sociology. 'Inside' view is 'mechanical', and 'outside' is epistemological and structural. The 'mechanical' is more popular today, but Khare prefers for having the epistemological and structural view due to scientific and humanistic considerations.[157]

In a recent comprehensive review of 'Trends in Indian Sociology', Ramkrishna Mukherjee reiterates his point of view, namely, diagnostic perspective about Indian sociology.[158] The main questions are:

1. What is it? (enumeration of the phenomenon)

2. How is it? (classification)
3. Why is it? (causality)
4. What will it be? (probability)
5. What should it be? (desirability)

These five questions should be related in a sequential manner with a dialectical appreciation, having both positive and negative points in regard to the reality of phenomena. These questions refer to *descriptive, explanatory, diagnostic* and *prescriptive* explanations. All questions do not have equal weight and emphasis.[159]

R.K.M. provides a bibliography, containing 712 references and surprisingly all these are cited in the text. He traces history of sociology as a profession from 1920s till 1970s [160] He also refers to a typology of the pre-professional stage of the intellectuals.[161] The sociologists are classified as (a) pioneers (1920s–40s), (b) modernizers (1950s), (c) insiders (1960s), (d) pace-makers (1970s), and (e) non-conformists (1970s). He analyses a selected few from each category on the basis of the variables of value-preference, theoretical orientation, research orientation and contribution to sociology. R.K.M. claims that his diagnostic approach would bridge up the gap between theory and research and integrate value and fact, and also a deductive-positivistic nature of sociology would be replaced by the inductive-inferential orientation[162]

In the end, a few words about methodological orientations in Indian sociology. We have already debated 'inside' view and/or 'outside' view, positivistic vs Indological orientation, diachronic vs synchronic approaches and other points, including a *nationalist* view of methodological orientation in Indian sociology. Methodology comprises of logic of enquiry and philosophy of science, techniques of operationalization of concepts and tools of research, problems of measurement and observation, and finally questions of universality and particularity in tools of research that use symbolic-linguistic categories for measurement and observation.[163] The concepts of methodology raise similar ideological issues and ethical questions of communication of values to the respondents and their use for desired goals of research. We often mention that 'participant observation' has come from Malinowski and Radcliffe-Brown's functionalism, 'village studies' from

American anthropology, 'Indology' from Weber and Dumont and 'history' from Marx as a method of study.

The basic question is: Whether methods and techniques used in Indian sociology reflect the researcher's consciousness about research goals and refer to the character of the research objects or that it is a borrowed research instrument without referring either to research as such or to the objects of research? It is necessary to ask this question when we set our eyes on the use of participant observation, questionnaire and schedule, cybernetic model, set-theory, mathematical models, survey designs, and historical-structural and comparative frameworks.

T.N. Madan, in a trend report on research methodology,[164] covers the period from 1950 to 1970. Madan looks at methodology from the point of analytic power, objectivity and explanation, methods, techniques and tools, and analysis of data in social research. Madan also discusses the views of Radhakamal Mukerjee, D.P. Mukerji and A.K. Saran, along with Dumont, Bailey and Srinivas. The 'inside' view vs 'outside' view finds a prominent place in Madan's review. However, Madan bases his analysis on the studies of tribes, castes, village communities, family, urban centres, population studies, etc. based on a number of books and articles, published in five well-known Indian journals of sociology.

Not much has been written on the craft of sociology and social anthropology. Madan and Beteille have edited a volume on field experiences and encounters of social anthropologist.[165] I.P. Desai's two articles, in *Economic and Political Weekly* – 'Craft of Sociology in India: An Autobiographical Perspective',[166] are really refreshing and enrich our understanding of Indian sociology. Desai mentions three points about the early phase of Indian sociology:

1. Methodology as a separate course was not learnt by any one of the sociologists of the second generation from Bombay University.
2. Sociology was not understood as a science as it is understood today.
3. Sociology was supposed to have a bearing on practical life and was future-oriented, that is, change-oriented.[167]

Desai's observations on the construction and use of questionnaire, sampling and tabulation, or in fact, on survey research are really illuminating. Desai and Srinivas represented two different traditions in Indian sociology in the 1950s at the University of Baroda. Srinivas was against the techniques of questionnaire and schedule, and use of statistics. Srinivas' strong point was his emphasis on field-work method. Desai is against any kind of borrowed theories, concepts and research tools. His writings amply show this orientation.

The new research technology in India has come due to constraints of Indian sociology itself and not due to any particular individuals. We shall take up a few points in detail in the chapters on the village studies and the studies on social stratification. An assumed international reference model of social science and the slow pace of Indian social transformation have conditioned the character and evaluation of Indian social science in general, and sociology and social anthropology in particular.

Notes

1. Yogendra Singh, 'Scope and Method of Sociology in India', in T.K.N. Unnithan, et al. (eds), *Sociology for India,* New Delhi: Prentice Hall of India, 1967, pp. 13–37; and 'Sociology for India: The Emerging Perspective', in ibid., pp. 165–183. See also Yogendra Singh, 'Disciplinary Growth of Sociology and its Teaching in India', in *Sociology in India,* Agra: Institute of Social Sciences, Agra University, 1965, pp. 53–67.
2. Ramkrishna Mukherjee, 'Trends in Indian Sociology', *Current Sociology,* Vol. 25, No. 3, 1977.
3. R.S. Khare, "Inside' Apropos of 'Outside': Some Implications of Sociological Debate', in Giri Raj Gupta (ed.) *Main Currents in Indian-Sociology,* Vol. I, New Delhi: Vikas Publishing House, 1976, pp. 20–58.
4. Louis Dumont and D.F. Pocock, 'For a Sociology of India', *Contributions to Indian Sociology* Vol. I, 1957, pp. 9–22.
5. Ibid., p. 9.
6. Ibid., p. 9.
7. R.N. Saxena, 'A Sociology in India', in *Sociology in India,* op. cit., 1965, pp. 1–13.

8. L. Dumont and D.F. Pocock, op. cit., p. 11.
9. Ibid., p. 11.
10. Ibid., p. 12.
11. Ibid., p. 12.
12. Ibid., p. 12.
13. Ibid., p. 13.
14. Ibid., p. 13.
15. Ibid., p. 13.
16. Ibid., p. 13.
17. F.G. Bailey, 'For a Sociology of India?', *Contributions to Indian Sociology,* No. III, 1959, pp. 88–101.
18. L. Dumont and D.F. Pocock, op. cit., 1957, pp. 10–11.
19. F.G. Bailey, op. cit., 1959, p. 90.
20. Ibid., p. 89.
21. F.G. Bailey, *Caste and the Economic Frontier,* Manchester: Manchester University Press, 1957.
22. F.G. Bailey op. cit., 1959, p. 92.
23. Ibid., p. 96.
24. L. Dumont and D.F. Pocock, 'Kinship' (a review of Iravati Karve's Kinship Organization in India), in *Contributions to Indian Sociology,* Vol. 1, 1957, p. 64.
25. F.G, Bailey, op. cit., 1959, p. 97.
26. Ibid., p. 98.
27. Cf. from Bailey, op. cit., 1959, p. 98.
28. Y. Singh, *Modernization of Indian Tradition,* Delhi: Thompson Press (India) Ltd., 1973, p. 17.
29. F.G. Bailey, op. cit., 1959, p. 98.
30. Ibid., pp. 98–99.
31. L. Dumont and D.F. Pocock, 'Village Studies', *Contributions to Indian Sociology,* No. 1, 1957, p. 41.
32. F.G. Bailey, op. cit., 1959, p. 99.
33. Ibid., p. 99.
34. Ibid., p. 100.
35. Ibid., p. 100.
36. Ibid., p. 100.

37. Ibid., p. 100.
38. L. Dumont and D.F. Pocock, 'For a sociology of India: a rejoinder to Dr. Bailey', *Contributions to Indian Sociology,* No. 4, 1960.
39. See, A.K. Saran's 'A Review of Contributions to Indian Sociology, No. IV', *Eastern Anthropologist,* Vol. XV, No. 1, 1962.
40. T.N. Madan, 'For a sociology of India', *Contributions to Indian Sociology,* No. IX, 1966, pp. 9–16.
41. L. Dumont responds to A.K. Saran's criticisms and T.N. Madan's 'weak' defence of their (Dumont and Pocock's) position, in 'A Fundamental Problem in the Sociology of Caste', *Contributions to Indian Sociology,* No. IX, 1966, pp. 17–32.
42. L. Dumont and D.F. Pocock, op. cit., 1960.
43. Ibid., p. 84.
44. T.N. Madan, op. cit., 1966, p. 12.
45. A.K. Saran, op. cit., 1962 p. 68.
46. T.N. Madan, op. cit., 1966, p. 12.
47. L. Dumont, op. cit., 1966, p. 22.
48. T.N. Madan, op. cit., 1966, pp. 11–12.
49. L. Dumont, op. cit., 1966, (fn. 9), p. 23.
50. A.K. Saran, op. cit., 1962, p. 68.
51. Imtiaz Ahmad, 'For a Sociology of India', *Contributions to Indian Sociology* (New Series), No. 4, 1972, p. 23.
52. L. Dumont, op. cit., 1966, p. 23.
53. Ibid., p. 23.
54. Ibid., p. 23.
55. Ibid., p. 24.
56. Ibid, p. 25.
57. T.N. Madan, 'For a Sociology of India: Some Clarifications', *Contributions to Indian Sociology (New Series),* 1967, pp. 90–93.
58. See, Emile Durkheim and Marcel Mauss, *Primitive Classifications* (Translated from French into English by Rodney Needham), London: 1963, and A.M. Hocart, *Caste, A Comparative Study,* London: Mathew & Co., 1950.
59. J.H. Hutton, *Caste in India,* Bombay (now Mumbai), Oxford University Press, 1963.
60. See, K.L. Sharma, *Essays on Social Stratification,* Jaipur, Rawat Publications, 1980, pp. 1–25.

61. L. Dumont, op. cit., 1966, pp. 25–26.
62. L. Dumont and D.F. Pocock, 'A Farewell', *Contributions to Indian Sociology,* No. IX, 1966, pp. 7–8.
63. J.P. Singh Uberoi, 'Science and Swaraj', *Contributions to Indian Sociology,* (NS), No. II, 1968, p. 119.
64. M.N. Srinivas, *Social Change in Modern India,* Berkeley: California University Press, 1966.
65. J.P. Singh Uberoi, op. cit., 1968, p. 120.
66. Ibid., p. 120.
67. Y. Singh, 'For a Sociology of India', *Contributions to Indian Sociology* (NS), No. 4, 1970, pp. 140–144.
68. Robert K. Merton, *Social Theory and Social Structure,* Glencoe: The Free Press, 1962.
69. Y. Singh, op. cit., 1970, p. 142.
70. D. Kantowsky, 'For a Sociology of India: A Critical Note on The Sociology of Developing Countries', *Contributions to Indian Sociology* (NS), No. 3, 1969, pp. 128–131.
71. Y. Singh, op. cit., 1970, p. 142.
72. Ibid., p. 142.
73. Ibid., p. 143.
74. Dhirendra Narain, 'For a Sociology of India: Some Observations', *Contributions to Indian Sociology* (NS), No. V, 1971, p. 131.
75. Ibid., pp. 131–132.
76. Ibid., p. 132.
77. Ibid., p. 133.
78. Ibid., p. 133.
79. T.N. Madan, 'For a Sociology of India', *Contributions to Indian Sociology,* (NS), Vol. 15, Nos. 1 and 2, 1981, pp. 403–418.
80. Y. Singh, op. cit. 1973: See also Y. Singh, 'The Role of Social Sciences in India: A Sociology of Knowledge', *Sociological Bulletin,* Vol. 22, No. 1, 1973, pp. 14–28.
81. Ramkrishna Mukherjee, 'Indian Sociology: Historical Development and Present Problems', *Sociological Bulletin,* Vol. 22, No. I, 1973, pp. 29–58. See also Ramkrishna Mukherjee, op. cit., 1977.
82. Y. Singh, 'Ideology, Theory and Methods in Indian Sociology', Stein Rokkan (ed.), *A Quarter Century of International Social Science,* New Delhi: Concept Publishing House, 1979, pp. 291–314.
83. Ibid., p. 292.

84. Ibid., p. 293.
85. T.N. Madan, op. cit., 1966.
86. Radhakamal Mukerjee, *The Philosophy of Social Science,* Delhi: Macmillan Co., 1960.
87. A.R. Desai's *Social Background of Indian Nationalism,* 1948, is referred in this context.
88. Y. Singh, op. cit., 1979.
89. See Y. Singh, op. cit., 1979.
90. See Ibid., pp. 298–301.
91. Ibid., pp. 301–304.
92. Ibid., pp. 304–306.
93. Ibid., pp. 306–309.
94. See, Yogendra Singh, op. cit., (1967), 'Caste and Class: Some Aspects of Continuity and Change', *Sociological Bulletin,* Vol. XVIII, No. 2, 1968, p. 2 and pp. 165–186; and op. cit., 1973, 1974 and 1979.
95. Y. Singh, *Modernization of Indian Tradition,* op. cit., 1973.
96. See, Y. Singh's 'Sociology of Social Stratification', in *A Survey of Research in Sociology and Social Anthropology,* Vol. I (ICSSR), Bombay: Popular Prakashan, 1974.
97. Y. Singh, 'Concepts and Theories of Social Change', in *A Survey of Research in Sociology and Social Anthropology,* Vol. I (ICSSR), Ibid.
98. Y. Singh, *Sociological Bulletin,* op. cit., 1973.
99. Ibid., p. 15.
100. Ibid., p. 18.
101. Ibid., p. 20.
102. Ibid., p. 20.
103. Ibid., p. 22.
104. T.N. Madan, op. cit., 1966.
105. Y. Singh, *Sociological Bulletin,* op. cit., 1973, p. 23.
106. Ibid., p. 23.
107. Ibid., p. 26.
108. Ibid., p. 26.
109. Ibid., pp. 27–28.
110. Y. Singh, op. cit., 1967, pp. 13–37.
111. See, for example, M.N. Srinivas and M.N. Panini, 'The Development of Sociology and Social Anthropology in India', *Sociological Bulletin,*

Vol. 22, No. 2; 1973, pp. 199-215; M.N. Srinivas, 'Sociology and Sociologists in India Today', *Sociological Bulletin,* Vol. XIX, No. 1, 1970, pp. 1–10. See also C. Lakshmanna, 'Teaching and Research in Sociology in India', *Sociological Bulletin,* Vol. 23, No. 1, 1974, pp. 1–13; Ramkrishna Mukherjee, 'The Sociologist and the Social Reality', *Sociological Bulletin,* Vol. 23, No. 2, 1974, pp. 169–192; S.C. Dube, 'Indian Sociology at the Turning Point', *Sociological Bulletin,* Vol. 26, No. 1, 1977, pp. 1–13, R.N. Saxena (ed.) *Sociology, Social Research and Social Problems in India,* Bombay, Asia Publishing House, 1961; and M.S.A. Rao, 'Sociology in the 1980s', *Economic and Political Weekly,* Vol. XIV, No. 44, 1974, pp. 1810–1815.

112. Ramkrishna Mukherjee, *The Rise and Fall of the East India Company,* Berlin: Academic Verlag, 1958.
113. Ramkrishna Mukherjee, *Dynamics of a Rural Society,* Berlin: Akademie-Verlag, 1957.
114. Ramkrishna Mukherjee, 'Study of Social Change and Social Development in the Developing Societies', *Economic and Political Weekly,* Vol. V, Nos. 29–31, 1970, pp. 1159–1170.
115. Ibid., p. 1161.
116. Ibid., p. 1161.
117. Ibid., p. 1163.
118. See, Ramkrishna Mukherjee, *Sociological Bulletin,* op. cit., 1973 and 1974.
119. Ramkrishna Mukherjee, *Sociological Bulletin,* op. cit., 1973, p. 29.
120. Ibid., p. 31.
121. Ibid., pp. 39–47.
122. Ramkrishna Mukherjee, op. cit., 1974, pp. 169–192.
123. Ibid., pp. 182–183.
124. D.P. Mukerji, *Diversities,* Delhi: People's Publishing House, 1958.
125. Gunnar Myrdal, *Asian Drama: An Inquiry into the Poverty of Nations,* Vol. I, Penguin Books, 1968.
126. Ramkrishna Mukherjee, op. cit., 1974, pp. 185–186.
127. P.C. Joshi, 'Reflections on Social Science Research in India', *Sociological Bulletin,* Vol. 24, No. 2, 1975, pp. 139–162.
128. Gunnar Myrdal, op. cit., 1968.
129. A.R. Desai, *Social Background of Indian Nationalism,* Bombay: Popular Prakashan, 1948.
130. P.C. Joshi, op. cit., 1975, p. 147.
131. Stanislaw Andreski, *Social Sciences as Sorcery,* New York: St. Martinus Press, 1972.

132. Jayant K. Lele, 'Indian Sociology and Sociology in India: Some Reflections on Their Being', *Sociological Bulletin,* Vol. 30, No. I, 1981, pp. 39–53.

133. A.R. Desai, op. cit., 1948.

134. See, A.R. Desai, *State and Society in India: Essays in Dissent,* Bombay: Popular Prakashan, 1975.

135. A.R. Desai, 'Relevance of the Marxist Approach to the Study of Indian Society', *Sociological Bulletin,* Vol. 30, No. 1, 1981, pp. 1–20.

136. Ibid., pp. 4–7.

137. Ibid., p. 11.

138. A.R. Desai, op. cit., 1948.

139. Louis Dumont, 'Nationalism and Communalism', *Contributions to Indian Sociology,* Vol. VII, 1964, p. 32.

140. Y. Singh, *Modernization of Indian Tradition,* op. cit., 1973.

141. H.C. Srivastava, 'Concept of Tradition in Indian Sociological Thought', *Social Scientist,* Vol. 3, No. 3, 1974, pp. 17–25.

142. Sumit Chopra, 'Old Wine in New Skins: Modernization of Indian Tradition', *Social Scientist,* Vol. 3, No. 4, 1974, pp. 78–84.

143. Ramkrishna Mukherjee, 'History and Tradition in Indian Society: Null and Alternate Hypotheses?', *Sociological Bulletin,* Vol. 24, No. 1, 1975, pp. 95–107.

144. Krishna Prakash Gupta, 'Sociology of Indian Tradition and Tradition of Indian Sociology', *Sociological Bulletin,* Vol. 23, No. 1, 1974, pp. 14–43.

145. Ibid., p. 37.

146. Ibid., p. 37.

147. Ibid., p. 37.

148. Ibid., p. 37.

149. D.A. Chekki, 'The Sociology of Sociologists: An Empirical Study in the Sociology of Knowledge', *Sociological Bulletin,* Vol. 27, No. 2, 1978, pp. 131–153. See also T.B. Bottomore, 'Sociology in India'. *British Journal of Sociology,* Vol. 13, June 1962, pp. 98–106; M.B. Clinard and J.W. Elder, 'Sociology in India: A Study in the Sociology of Knowledge', *American Sociological Review,* Vol. 30, August 1965, pp. 581–587; and R.N. Mukherjee and H. Mujumdar, 'Sociology in India', in H. Becker and H.E. Barnes (eds), *Social Thought from Lore to Science,* Vol. 2, Washington DC: Harren Press, pp. 1135–1148.

150. A.R. Momin, 'Indian Sociology: Search for Authentic Identity', *Sociological Bulletin*, Vol. 27, No. 2, 1978, p. 169.
151. Indra Deva, 'Methodological Perspectives for the Study of Society', in Giri Raj Gupta (ed.), op. cit., 1976, pp. 75–98.
152. R.S. Khare, op. cit., 1976, pp. 19–58.
153. Ibid., p. 23.
154. Ibid., p. 24.
155. Ibid., p. 38
156. Ibid., p. 39.
157. Ibid., pp. 52–57.
158. R.K. Mukherjee, op. cit., 1977.
159. Ibid., pp. 2–5.
160. Ibid., p. 18.
161. Ibid., p. 12.
162. Ibid., pp. 37–43.
163. Y. Singh, op. cit., 1979.
164. T.N. Madan, 'Research Methodology', in *A Survey of Research in Sociology and Social Anthropology*, Vol. 3 (ICSSR), Bombay: Popular Prakashan, pp. 282–315.
165. T.N. Madan and Andre Beteille (eds), *Encounter and Experience*, Delhi: Vikas, 1975.
166. I.P. Desai, 'Craft of Sociology in India: An Autobiographical Perspective', *Economic and Political Weekly*, Vol. XVI, No. 6, pp. 197–204 and Vol. XVI, No. 7, pp. 246–251.
167. Ibid., p. 197.

Chapter 4

Studies on Social Stratification

A Sociology of Knowledge Perspective

Studies on social stratification in India reflect the same theory, method and data which we find in regard to the studies on other aspects of Indian society. Social stratification is a very sensitive field of study. The people, the researchers and the governmental agents (leaders and bureaucrats) are parts of the system of social stratification. The people are divided into different caste, class, occupational, professional and power groups or categories. The researchers are a part of these divisions and study of social stratification by them may bring in subjectivity in understanding of positions of others vis-á-vis their own positions.

The government of India has a policy about the nature of social groupings and categories of groups and relations between them. The criticisms of the government are that its policy and action have been at variance; that the rich are becoming richer and the poor are becoming poorer; and that social inequality is 'officially' institutionalized and this speaks about the nature of the ruling classes and power elites. Thus, social stratification is a field of study which demands a critical analysis from the point of sociology of knowledge. Theory, method and data are the three main concerns in the present study.

A large number of studies on 'caste' have been brought out during the past half a century (between 1930s and 1980s). A few studies have been published on 'class', particularly in the 1970s.

Some scholars have focussed on the three 'orders', namely, social, economic and political, in their studies on social stratification taking clues from Max Weber[1] and P.A. Sorokin.[2] Our objective is not to provide a chronology of the studies on caste, class and social stratification. The main aim of our study is to analyse these studies from the point of their theory, method and data.

Y. Singh has analysed the studies on social stratification and social change[3] conducted in the 1950s and 1960s from the point of sociology of knowledge. Singh has analysed the studies on social stratification conducted in the 1970s.[4] It would, therefore, be desirable to give a brief resume of Singh's analysis of the studies on social stratification in the 1950s, 1960s and 1970s.

The Main Questions in the Studies on Social Stratification

The issues in the sociology of social stratification relate to questions of theory, structure and process of social stratification.[5] Singh writes: 'The theory of social stratification implies a set of concepts, propositions and assumptions that are verified and validated and constitute an explanatory system.'[6] Singh observes that studies on social stratification rarely reach the formal level of theory. The two well-known orientations in the studies on social stratification are of 'functional' and 'conflict' theories. Singh refers to a couple of attempts made by sociologists towards a synthesis of the functional and the conflict theories. He observes: 'Now the increasing tendency is to analyse social stratification from a pluralistic conceptual frame by treating both conflict and consensus as two dimensions of the same reality.'[7] But Singh does not make this statement in regard to the studies on social stratification in India. Referring to Hans Zetterberg's distinction between the 'propositional' and the 'dimensionalistic' theory in sociology,[8] Singh mentions 'status, wealth, power' approach to the study of social stratification as this corresponds to the 'dimensionalistic' theory. The 'theory' of social stratification thus refers to 'why' of social stratification.

The 'structure' of social stratification could be seen in two ways: (a) the nominalist and (b) the realist.[9] The nominalism refers to role or status as the unit of social stratification. Davis and Moore and Parsons[10] (the well-known functionalists) consider 'positions' and 'roles' as the units of social stratification. Certain 'attributes' are the basis of classification of roles and positions. Social classes, elites, status groups or castes are taken as units in the realist frame of analysis.[11] The processes of social stratification are seen as 'changes in the differentiation, evaluation, ranking and rewarding patterns.'[12] Accretion, transformation and replacement are the consequences of the processual nature of social stratification. The questions which Singh has posed in regard to theory, structure and process of social stratification are as follows:

1. What theoretical assumptions have guided studies in social stratification in India?
2. How far have the functional or dialectical (conflict) theoretical postulates been used either for analysis or selection of problems in social stratification?
3. Which are the major structural foci in social stratification studies, and has the focus been comprehensive enough to cover most strategic structural units or components of the system of stratification?
4. Or has the focus been biassed for historical or other disciplinary reasons towards studies in a specific or particular direction?
5. Have these studies been sociologically relevant?
6. Do these studies focus upon the most strategic processes of social stratification?
7. Have the studies highlighted in a representative manner the processes of social stratification, their causes, consequences and impact upon the overall social order and change in the Indian social system?[13]

Singh analyses 'caste system and social stratification,' 'scheduled castes and social stratification,' 'class structures and social stratification,' 'agrarian class stratification and change,' and 'elites and social stratification' in India in the first 'trend report' published in 1974.[14] The studies in the 1950s and 1960s have been grouped under these headings.

In the trend report, 'Sociology of Social Stratification in India-II',[15] Singh provides a sharper analysis of sociology of knowledge perspective about social stratification. The headings are evidence of the concern for the sociology of knowledge perspective. The main points are: ideological debate, changing theoretical orientations, structuralist approach, structural-historical approach, Marxist analysis of social stratification, other social sciences and stratification, social stratification in non-Hindu communities, tribes and scheduled castes, and sociology and social change. These points compared to the points in the earlier trend report are definitely indicative of change in the theoretic orientations and themes of study in social stratification. Singh clearly exposes the sociology of knowledge perspective for studying social stratification in India.

New theoretical and substantive issues in the studies on social stratification in the 1970s have come up due to self- awareness of Indian sociologists. New social situation and evaluation of the national ideology of social stratification have led to the emergence of self-criticism and search for relevance among the Indian sociologists.[16] Singh identifies the following new trends in the studies of social stratification:

1. increased debates on the ideological moorings of concepts and theories;
2. efforts to re-schematize conceptual systems and their presuppositions in the light of shifting paradigms;
3. the new substantive concerns in stratification studies; and finally
4. fruitful convergence of multi-disciplinary interests, both substantive and theoretical, in the studies of social stratification.[17]

The colonial background of the methodological and theoretical legacy of social sciences was attacked along with sociological positivism of the West. The quest for indigenization of paradigms and for relevance[18] became a focal point of attention among Indian social scientists. A broad framework of sociology of knowledge was rooted into experiential reality of Indian society and its historicity. The shadow of colonialism and positivism has been haunting Indian sociology for a long time. Why its harmful impact is realized in the 1970s and not in the 1950s and the 1960s is a question to be examined, carefully.

Concepts and frameworks given by the British scholars during India's colonization and by the American social scientists in the 1950s and 1960s have led to perpetuation of colonization, academic and intellectual dependency and mystification of knowledge.[19] A serious 'rethinking' is required. It is not true that all the sociologists and social anthropologists were influenced by American sociological positivism or British functionalism. Iravati Karve's work on kinship,[20] I.P. Desai's study of family,[21] A.R. Desai's study of nationalism,[22] and some other scholars remained unaffected by Western theoretical and methodological thinking. However, departments of sociology at the universities of Delhi: Jaipur and Chandigarh have had the imprints of such influences.[23]

The crux of the ideological debate is that the concepts, frameworks and paradigms which have dominated the academics are being challenged, refuted and revised or replaced. Mencher suggests that caste be studied from the 'upside down' rather than 'top down' perspective.[24] Use of historical material is emphasized by Saberwal.[25] Sharma pleads for structural-historical perspective accepting Indian society as a 'social formation'.[26] The bias of the elite upper caste and class sociologists in their studies has been highlighted.[27] An alternative perspective is offered in the form of a shift of emphasis. Caste model of Indian society[28] is being questioned. The question of evolution of caste and class in India is again looked at afresh by Myrdal,[29] Klass[30] and Sinha.[31] Arguments of Srinivas and Dumont regarding 'sociology for India' are considered not only irrelevant but also harmful.[32] They are blamed for putting wrong priorities and emphasis in sociological studies.

The Theoretical Orientations

Y. Singh classifies the theoretic concerns in the stratification studies of the 1970s as: (a) structural-functional, (b) structuralist, (c) structural-historical, and (d) historical-materialist or Marxist. During the 1950s, there was dominance of the structural-functional theory of stratification. Towards the end of the 1950s, structuralism and Marxism emerged in the studies of social stratification. In the 1970s the historical perspective was adopted by both Marxists and non-Marxists.

Before we take up the studies on social stratification for our analysis, it may be noted that the evolution of approaches to stratification cannot, in fact, be characterized only by structural-functionalism in the 1950s, structuralism and Marxism in the 1960s, and structural-historical (both Marxists and non-Marxists) in the 1970s. Structural-historical perspective was adopted by A.R. Desai,[35] a noted Marxist, in 1940s; structuralist view could be seen in the 1950s in the writings of Bougiel,[36] Dumont[37] and Hocart.[38] The 1950s and 1960s were dominated by both structural-functionalism (both American and British) and structuralism[39] (both British and French). Structural-historical perspective has ideological overtones of both borrowed and modified Marxism and indigenization in the form of a reaction to Marxist perspective and rejection of Western positivism and culturology.[40] Even today, there are people engaged in studies from the point of Western positivism, culturologism and orthodox Marxism.[41]

K.L. Sharma divides the studies on stratification into two categories: (a) the studies on caste stratification; and (b) the multi-dimensional studies.[42] The studies in the first category are by Kroeber, Weber, Hutton, Ghurye, Hocart, Myrdal, Dumont, Leach, Srinivas, Dube, Bailey, Lewis, Mayer, Mathur, Majumdar, Marriott, etc.[43] These sociologists and social anthropologists have focussed on caste as the sole institution of social ranking. What is known as 'caste model of Indian society' is their theoretical perspective. Caste is treated as an extreme form of class or as a closed community. Others have given premium to socio-religious and ritualistic considerations. The ideas related to pollution-purity and religion are treated as the basis of caste ranking. 'Elaboration' of caste ranking has also been compared in various zones of India. None of these studies refer to the phenomena of class and power. They, in fact, consider caste as synonym with social structure. These studies were carried out in the 1950s and in the first half of the 1960s.

The multidimensional studies on social stratification do not consider caste as an all-inclusive basis of social stratification. Economic position, style of life, education, occupation and personality attributes are evaluated for assessing a person's rank in his community or caste. Beteille refers to the emergence of 'differentiated institutional structures of various kinds' and 'caste free' areas.[44] Later on, he explains the necessity for studying 'ideas and interests'.[45] One finds a shift in Beteille's emphasis from 'caste-oriented' studies to 'class-oriented' studies of stratification. Bhatt's study of caste, class and politics[46] and Aggarwal's study of caste, religion and power[47] also emphasize the multidimensionality of social stratification. However, studies by Gough[48] and Kamakrishna Mukherjee[49] are different in theoretic orientation, compared to the studies by Bateille, Bhatt and Aggarwal. Gough and Mukherjee look at caste from a class point of view, with Marxist disposition. But it is clear that even in the 1960s 'caste alone' view was questioned. Sharma's study of six villages in Rajasthan[50] in the 1960s highlighted the role of ascription, units of ranking, dimensions of stratification, ideological bases of stratification, factors of change in stratification and its emerging patterns. Both 'structural' and 'cultural' perspectives were used to facilitate an analysis of caste, class, caste and class consciousness, occupational and social mobility, power-structure and value-orientation. Land-tenure systems, land reforms, Panchayati Raj, educational achievements, occupational opportunities and networks were studied in particular, in view of the multidimensionality of social stratification and limitations of the 'caste model' for studying Indian society.

The studies of social stratification in the 1950s and 1960s were guided by structural-functionalism and structuralism, barring a few studies which had variants of structural-historical perspective. Y. Singh observes that the basic premises of structural-functional studies have implied a *systemic teleology* based on the Brahminic or 'hierarchical' model of caste society, harmony or consensus as the system, from which change, differentiation or fission was studied, and the emphasis was on a micro-structural or communitarian scale of reality.[51] The caste system would not change. It would absorb all tensions and changes generated by polity and economy. 'Summation of roles' was its basic feature, hence consensual ideology. Historicity was a casualty in these studies of caste system.[52] However, the structural-functional studies in the 1970s have shown two tendencies: (a) deeper substantive and theoretical concerns in respect of processes of change, and (b) increased diagnostic orientation.[53] The notions of social mobility advanced by Srinivas[54] have been examined afresh. Downward mobility, proletarianization and bourgeoisiefication as processes of structural charge[55] have been reported. Relations between caste and class, caste and religion, caste and tribe etc. have also been questioned. Dumont and Srinivas have ideologized (in their differing characteristic styles) resilience of the caste system and its principle of hierarchy.[56] Bailey,[57] Kolenda[58] and Miller[59] refer to changes in the caste system from its 'organic' nature to its 'segmentary' character, but hold the view that caste continues to be the focal point of hierarchical relations in Indian society.

Let us take up a few studies from the point of their theoretical positions. Srinivas' emphasis on the role of religion in the Coorg society is clearly an extension of Radcliffe-Brown's functionalism. Srinivas observes that everything could be seen in terms of pure and impure. The entire life is organized around religion. Thus, it is the social organization of religion that encompasses everything else. Srinivas does not look at the polity, economy, consequences of religion on people's existence, etc. as the points necessary for investigation.

The Weberian Approach

Srinivas' perspective has inspired several scholars for undertaking their doctoral researches on similar lines. However, some students of Srinivas have differed from him. Beteille's study of social stratification in a village in Tamil Nadu may be cited here.[60] Beteille poses the question: 'What is the central theme of the study here presented?' He answers this question by saying: 'Broadly speaking, our concern is with the phenomena of caste, class and power with their changing relations.'[61] Beteille refers to 'caste-free' areas. He writes: 'The social system has acquired a much more complex and dynamic character, now there is a tendency for cleavages to cut across one another.' 'The hierarchies of caste, class, and power in the village overlap to some extent, but also cut across.'[62] Beteille justifies his use of the concept of 'class' as he finds 'the differentiation of institutional structures'. Weber's notion of class is found useful to understand emergence of market economy. Beteille's perspective is also evident when he states that '... there is a very little pre-occupation with purity, pollution, and rituals in general.'[63]

This is a qualitatively different position compared with that of Srinivas. Beteille not only treats caste, class and power as abstract categories on the pattern of 'class, status and party' as given by Weber, he also finds diversity at empirical level between economic, social and political distinctions among the people.

The problem with Beteille's formulation is not that distinctions are not there, but apriori acceptance of Weber's theory and its implicit ideology creates problems in proper understanding of social reality in a village of Tamil Nadu. Methodological individualism, Verstehen or interpretative understanding and rationalism (or psychologism) are fundamental bases of Weber's triology (class, status and party). These are neither stated nor exemplified by adopting certain research strategies. Surreptitious adoption of Weber's schema is evident in Beteille's study. Diversity between Indian village and German society (which was basis of Weber's formulation) is overlooked. Application of Weber's approach for studying social stratification by Beteille implies a contradiction between theory and method.[64]

There are two more studies, one by P.C. Aggarwal[65] and other by Anil Bhatt,[66] which may be treated along with Beteille's study discussed above. Aggarwal also does not formulate his theoretical proposition like Beteille; however, we can draw from it some of the statements and data reported in Aggarwal's study. Let me also mention that Aggarwal's study is more of a village monograph rather than a study of social stratification based on caste, religion and power. He has studied the Meos of Mewat with a holistic perspective. Meos are a Muslim community. Structural-functional orientation is implicit as Aggarwal gives a detailed account of the region, the people, the village, caste system, economic life, family and kinship, religion, life cycle rites and political organization. Some historical glimpses have also been provided. Participant observation and unstructured interviews were used for gathering data. Scaling technique was also used in analysing data. Meos' integration with the wider society and with the Hindus was also investigated.

Though Aggarwal uses ethnography as a methodological device, his emphasis is on the understanding of social structure of the Meos in Chavandi Kalan, a village in Alwar district of Rajasthan.

Aggarwal concludes that ritual status is insignificant in social ranking. Unequal distribution of power and economic resources is the crucial basis. However, Aggarwal's study lacks an understanding of 'class relations' among the Meos. Thus only inferentially, we consider Aggarwal's study as structural-functional, but in form as the title suggests, it is more based on Weberian perspective.

A clear exposition of theoretical formulation is found in Bhatt's study of caste, class and politics. He states that the objectives of his study are: (a) to compare and correlate ascriptive, socio-economic and political dimensions of social stratification; (b) to study the interaction between traditional social structures and modern democratic politics; and (c) to examine the extent to which the traditional model of social stratification in India obtains today.[67] The model of social stratification in traditional India is that of 'summation of statuses'. All aspects become subservient to the basis of this model. The implications of this model are that caste encompassed all other aspects; there was no differentiation within the caste groups; it was a homogenous but complex social organization, and there were non-antagonistic strata. Thus, the traditional India had closed, highly hierarchical, combinative, non-competitive social stratification.[68] Bhatt writes: 'For my purpose, the first view serves as a benchmark in contrast to the democratically ordered society envisioned by the constitution of independent India.'[69] Like 'comparative politics', Bhatt uses the phrase 'comparative social stratification.'[70] The writings which are cited by Bhatt are of Robert Dahl, L. Rudolph and S. Rudolph, Bernard Barber, McKim Marriott, Neil Smelser and S.M. Lipset, M. Tumin, A.C. Mayer, F. Barth, Andre Beteille, F.G. Bailey, Rajni Kothari and S. Verba and N. Pie, etc.[71] in support of his structural-functional perspective.

Bhatt puts the question: 'Can India realize this new order in such a deep-rooted and pervasive traditional social structure?' In view of this question, Bhatt explores relationship between society and politics. 'Social system is conceptualized as a larger system and political system as its subsystem.'[72] Bhatt's conceptual framework conceives of society as a separate and larger system instead of an aggregate of interacting subsystems. Such a framework considers social structures as independent variables and political factors as dependent variables.[73] Bhatt's study is an 'ideal' illustration of structural-functionalist positivism. Analysis of the pattern and degree of relationship between caste, class and politics, the degree of status-congruence, the extent of socio-economic and political inequalities, the degree of internal differentiation, the impact of caste status on socio-economic and political positions and conversely the impact of democratic political structures on processes of the caste system reveals the notion of 'whole' and 'parts' relationships. We shall refer to the methodological and substantive aspects of this study later on.

The Structural-Functional – Positivistic Approach

V.S. D'Souza applies the structural-functionalist positivistic approach to the study of social stratification in urban India. His study of Chandigarh and analysis of caste and class emphasize the significance of the continuum of the rigidity-fluidity dimensions and the individual, and his properties as the units of analysis, rather than castes as endogamous groups. Class and individual as the bases of social stratification in place of caste and group are considered significant in the present context. In his study of Chandigarh, D'Souza considers educational, occupational and income hierarchies as predominant features of urban social stratification. These are significantly related with each other. A scale of prestige is constructed based on these variables. Following L. Warner and Richard Centres, etc. D'Souza classifies classes as upper, middle, working class and lower class based on the prestige of individual members. The data are based on survey method and attitudinal responses. This approach is generally known as 'attributional' approach.

A crude copy of structural-functionalism is found in Rajni Kothari's study, *Politics in India*.[77] Kothari and Bhatt provide a similar perspective, however, their data base and research strategies are not the same. Kothari analyses politics at macro level, based on secondary sources, published researches and other materials. Bhatt's study is rooted into typical American sociological positivism, hence a comparative study based on sampling and questionnaire from four states of India. Structural-functionalism in

Kothari's study is evident from the following statements taken from the first chapter of his book:

1. India is a relatively open political system, hence no congruent development. Discrepancy between ideal and real creates inequalities including the political ones.
2. The social system in India provides a key to political stability. Any change in power relations should be seen in this perspective as well.
3. The traditional political culture seeks to incorporate into its womb the best elements of the culture of the modern world, without destroying the age-old traditions and diversities.
4. Thus, Indian society operates still largely as a political society.
5. Politics in India is pre-eminently the politics of *integration,* e.g. structural continuity exists in the sphere of power.[78]

Kothari refers to the processes of 'nation-building'. He writes: 'What is being stressed is the increasing political orientation of social interests, in which the political process provides the inclusive setting within which these interests are found to interact.'[79] However, this perspective of Kothari has been belied even before this was published. The elections of 1967 witnessed defeat of the Congress Party in more than half of the states. Of late, the emergence of regional forces and culture of politics in Tamil Nadu, Andhra Pradesh and Punjab[80] have also falsified the basic tenets of Kothari's thesis. What was not accepted said by Selig Harrison about the emergence of regional forces[81] perhaps could be accepted after the Akali movement in Punjab and the emergence of Telugu Desham in Andhra Pradesh.

Kothari uses the vocabulary of American 'functionalists' in particular, without inhibition or objection in both the volumes – *Politics in India* and in his 'Introduction: Caste in Indian Politics'.[82] We may refer a few statements to show the conservatism of fuctionalist approach vis-á-vis of Kothari. Kothari writes: 'Politics is a competitive enterprise, its purpose is the acquisition of power for the realisation of certain goals, and its process is one of identifying and manipulating existing and emerging allegiances in order to mobilise and consolidate positions.'[83] Politics is mass based. Politics must strive to organize through such a structure (caste structure).[84] *Politicization of caste* is necessary for modernizing India. Politics is an instrument for a group to consolidate its position.[85] Kothari accepts an American author's view – *'the democratic incarnation of caste,'*[86] Caste has the *secular aspect,*[87] it has the integration aspect, and the *aspect of consciousness.*[88] These aspects led to the *modernization* of India's polity.[89] Let us quote again: 'Finally, the politicization of caste makes for outward looking, upward moving orientations and as this results in the phenomenon of multiple memberships and overlapping identities, the result is highly secular for the polity as well as the society at large.'[90] This not only speaks of theoretical, methodological and epistemological apriorism and determinism, but also reveals an utter lack of understanding or realization of historicity of Indian society and polity. Kothari does not debate the relevance or irrelevance of the functionalist perspective before accepting it for studying Indian society. He does not compare it with alternative perspectives and frameworks. Such a quite acceptance of a theoretical perspective smacks of an academic conspiracy and ideological propaganda. We leave this debate at this point.

Let us now make a brief mention of two books, namely, F.G. Bailey's – *Caste and the Economic Frontier,*[91] and T.S. Epstein's – *Economic Development and Social Change in South India*[92]. Both of these studies focus on social change in villages, but the structural aspect of change is duly taken into account, and therefore, it would be relevant to make a reference about them. Bailey looks at the caste system in a village in Orissa (now Odisha) under a new economy. The new frontiers are economic and political and administrative. Transfer of land from the ex- landowners is a significant fact which makes land a market commodity, and other occupations which were tied with landlordism also become part of a market-situation. Bailey gives details about new economy, land transactions, services and trade. Bailey writes: 'The mercantile economy has impinged on the system of agriculture, because those who profited as merchants, traders and earners of salaries invested their money in land.'[93] Bailey puts three questions: (a) Why did they do so? (b) What made it possible for them to buy land? (c) What has been the effect of the redistribution of land on the social structure of the village? These are questions which support the position which Bailey took about Dumont and Pocock's position regarding Indian sociology. Bailey looks at 'culture' from the perspective of 'structure'.

Epstein's study of social change is guided by a comparative perspective. Epstein follows by and large Bailey's approach. The main argument of Epstein's study is that a structural innovation (economic development), namely, irrigation consolidates village economy, but it restricts social change, particularly, migration, contacts, education and politicization etc. Conversely, a lack of such an innovation results into widespread social change without corresponding economic development. Epstein's study of two villages in Karnataka based on the structural perspective provides details about crops, houses, landholdings, livestock, family incomes and expenditures, market networks, etc. Her study, like that of Bailey, focuses on change in the traditional social structure and hierarchy of the village community.

The Structuralist Approach

Levi-Strauss's structuralist principle of complimentary dualism or logical principle of opposition as a fundamental feature of human mind[94] is applied by Louis Dumont in his study of hierarchy and marriage alliance.[95] Pure and impure, consanguinity and affinity are examples of this logical dualism. These also refer to the notion of hierarchy. Graded statuses are entrenched into all spheres, including kinship. Dumont sees intercaste, intracaste and intrafamilial ranking as projections of the same intellectual and ideological principle. Dumont emphasized on the necessity of looking for *cultural meaning* of affinity and consanguinity. The structuralist stance of Dumont is clearly seen in his assertion that it is hierarchy which is a pervasive principle of Hindu society and the caste system is only one expression of it. There is a hierarchy of principles and values of occupations, food and clothes, and also of 'bride-givers' and 'bride-takers'.

It is this thinking of Dumont which he had about Indian society in the 1950s that found its fuller expression and exposition in his subsequent writings in *Contributions to Indian Sociology* and in *Homo Hierarchicus*.[96] Y. Singh observes that the pivotal notions of structuralism are: *ideology, dialectics, transformational relationship* and comparison in regard to social stratification as particularly found in Dumont's *Homo Hierarchicus.* The basic tenet of caste system is 'hierarchy'. The opposition between pure and impure defines its binary tension, its dialectics. Dumont observes that 'hierarchy also inheres the relationship of "encompassing" and being "encompassed".'[97]

Dumont's theoretical perspective is clear in the statement: 'I think that this view of the duality as one of form and content is mistaken, and that hierarchy, especially in its exemplary Indian form, teaches us a better way of looking at it.'[98] Dumont makes three points about this:

1. A hierarchical relation is a relation between larger and smaller, or more precisely, between *that which encompasses and that which is encompassed.* 'The duality that plagues us is not one of form and content but that of the *encompassing and the encompassed.*' The duality is real insofar as *we come to know* the two kinds of aspects in a different way: (a) basic values related to kinship, caste, status, etc. and (b) political or economic aspects as observed in actual situations.
2. Opposition is found between the orientation to the whole (holism) and the orientation to the element *(individualism*). Caste represents the holistic orientation and equality refers to the individualistic orientation. The 'whole' is something religious (or philosophical), while 'economy' is a matter of the individual. The division of labour in the Indian village is not an economic fact: it is a holistic (religious) fact.
3. The third point refers to ritual status and power. The king as sovereign is the high priest and the ruler in one person. It is a fact. But in *principle,* the priest and the king are absolutely distinguished – the priest is highest in status even if he is dependent, materially. Thus, priesthood encompasses rulership; and at the same time these 'twin forces' together encompass all the rest.[99]

Dumont's conception of social change or the principle of transformational relationship is moulded by his frame of reference. Dumont observes that there has been change *in* the society and not *of* the society. Dumont postulates that *comparison* is possible within a cultural type, it is also possible within such types. He does not emphasise on the uniqueness of a society. Comparison is possible between logically opposite types, hence comparison of India with West and vice versa.

Dumont's structuralist view on India's social stratification in terms of pure and impure or binary opposition (encompassing and encompassed) is found lacking, theoretically as well as substantively. The 'pure' is found in the 'impure,' and vice versa. Gould's concept of 'contrapriest'[100] explains the fusion of purity or priesthood in the 'impure' or 'untouchable'. In a symposium on Dumont's *Homo Hierarchicus*, it is suggested by Veena Das[101] and Das and J.P.S. Uberoi[102] that the pure and impure are fused in many rituals. It is suggested that the dichotomy of 'sacred' and 'non-sacred' and the notion of 'reciprocity' would be more appropriate for analysing caste system in India

Dumont's structuralist perspective lacks a conception of history.[103] His view also suffers from the neglect of the politico-economic dimensions of Indian reality.[104] However, Dumont makes a clear distinction between the substantivist and the structuralist modes of thinking. He draws a distinction between dialectics and hierarchy, contradiction and complementarity. Pure and impure are not of a dialectical nature; they are complementary opposites.[105] Y. Singh observes that Dumont's view has created a high self-consciousness among Indian sociologists about the study of caste and class in India.[106]

Some Alternative Perspectives

There are a few studies in which differentiation, evolution and change in caste and class over a period of time have been focussed. We could say that the emphasis in these studies could be seen as on caste, caste and class, class alone, again study of caste, and caste and class as parts of a social formation. Besides sociologists and social anthropologists, historians and economists have conducted studies from the structural-historical perspective, particularly of the agrarian and the industrial stratification systems, and mode of production in agriculture vis-á-vis rural class structure.

Mortan Klass[107] and S. Sinha[108] have analysed once again the origin and evolution of the caste system in India. The continuity of caste system has been possible mainly due to support of economic factors and internalization of the hierarchical norms among people. The question of origin of caste has also been raised by the Marxists, namely, S.A. Dange, B.T. Ranadive and E.M.S. Namboodiripad.[109] They all look at caste as an institution based on exploitation by the upper castes of the lower ones. Mencher sees caste as a form of class.[110] The non-Marxist scholars do not treat caste as a superstructural entity, whereas the Marxist scholars treat it as a superstructural phenomenon. The latter are certainly not correct, but the former also cannot ignore the role of economic forces in the evolution and resilience of the caste system.

A couple of studies of social and agrarian movements have been taken up with the non-Marxist structural-historical perspective, particularly by M.S.A. Rao,[111] Rajendra Singh,[112] P.N. Mukherji,[113] K.L Sharma.[114] The studies of caste and class relationship have been conducted by Saberwal,[115] S. Sivakumar and Chitra Siva Kumar are also networking.[116] All of them have emphasized on the element of *time* and the influences which economic, political and ideological forces had upon caste and class. These studies are 'historical', but they are different from those of historians, as they have studied neither the remote past nor the immediate one in details, based on primary sources. Most of these studies are of contemporary period and cover a vast canvas. They refer more to 'levels' and 'breakthroughs' for getting insights into the emergence of the present structures. Thus, the historically-oriented studies give emphasis on the understanding of the present by conducting field studies. Y. Singh also shows his preference for structural-historical approach.[117]

Y. Singh outlines the main features of the Marxist analysis of social stratification as follows: 'The treatment of stratification in Marxist theory has distinctive features: it is systematic; it is dialectical; it treats structures (stratification) as historical product; it locates historical forces in the mode of production, reflection of the specific nature of man which under certain historical conditions creates contradictions of classes; it is essentially evolutionary and developmental, since mode of production and the relationship that it generates are endowed with dialectical quality of self transformation'.[110] Mode of production is the key of the Marxist theory of social stratification.

The systematic studies based on this approach began with A.R. Desai's study of 'nationalism' in the 1940s, but more of such studies have been taken up as a reaction to the studies based on structural-functional and structuralist approaches. Singh refers to the village studies by J. Pathi,[119] P.K. Bose,[120] Hira Singh,[121] D.N. Dhanagare,[122] D. Gupta,[123] and Kathleen Gough.[124]

The mode of production debate[125] highlights the issues related to nature of agrarian class structure and differentiation of peasantry. These studies refer to the forces and factors of class polarisation, exploitation, bourgeoisiefication of the peasantry and pauperisation of the rural working class. Thus, the basic concern is the study of origin, structure and change in caste and class in India.[126] Caste and kinship are analysed from a class point of view.[127] Caste is not treated as culture-specific system, but a reflection of class relationships.

Let us now refer to a few illustrative studies from the point of their conceptual framework. While analysing the social and economic structure of rural India, Bettelheim writes: 'Throughout its existence, the colonial system grafted new legal ties and property rights into the existing framework of production.'[128] The laws created privileged social classes and also enforced the status quo. Bettelheim analyses rural class structure in the post-independence period in view of Zamindari, Mahalwari Ryotwari and Jagirdari systems of land-tenure. Borrowing from D. Thorner,[129] Bettelheim analyses Mazdoors, Kisans and Maliks. The change is seen towards *capitalism.* In the same way, Bettelheim analyses India's industrial structure, the bourgeoisie and capital, the proletariat and the petty bourgeoisie, and the nature of Indian state. A similar analysis is found in a collection of essays by A.R. Desai.[130]

In a study of a village in Tamil Nadu, John Harris discusses the issue of capitalism and peasant farming.[131] He uses the Marxist approach with a difference. Harris writes: 'I argue that the expanded reproduction of capital in agricultural production is subordinated to that of merchant and finance capital, in a form of economy like those described by Marx as "intermediate" forms of capitalism. The process of "differentiation" of the peasantry is thus "blocked" both because of the character of the economy and by the ideological structures of caste and kinship which reinforce the existing relations of production and the power structure.'[132] Thus, Harris examines the question of relationship between caste and mode of production. Control of land by members of a caste is considered as a decisive determinant of 'dominance'. Harris finds that class of rich peasant-merchant-moneylenders came to dominate both agriculture and trade, and this is shown up in the dominance of the members of the same caste in both agriculture and trade.[133]

Some of the essays in an edited volume *Land, Caste and Politics in India* by Gail Omvedt,[134] clearly show that caste is not merely a cultural category. Atrocities on Harijans, movements of Dalits, unity moves among the Kulaks, indicate that the dominant castes are less of castes and more of classes. This amply shows class genesis of the social relations among people. Omvedt writes: 'Class should be basically defined in terms of the *social* as the Marxist concept of the social *relations of production*.'[135] Omvedt feels that 'caste is not only form but also concrete material content'.[136] The Indian feudal social formation was actually based on a *caste, feudal mode of production.* Castes and classes are found in a mix, and both have feudal and capitalist forms and affect each other, hence a social formation perspective.[137] Omvedt agrees with Gough's classification of the pre-British South Indian society into five major classes: (a) the 'state class'; (b) the 'state servants', (c) 'commodity producers and merchants', (d) 'peasants, herders, fishermen and attached village servants', and (e) 'agricultural and menial slaves'.[138] The last could be called Dalit labourers. The first four classes are seen as equivalent of four varnas, and the fifth with the untouchables.

K.L. Sharma writes: 'The understanding of caste and class demands an approach which, has: (a) dialectics, (b) history, (c) culture, and (d) structure, as its essential features.'[139] Dialectics do not mean binary tension, but imply a change through time as a result of contradictions. History gives an account of levels and events in the structure of society. Culture refers to the norms which define the patterns of relations. Structure is seen as a product of dialectical, historical and cultural forces. Therefore, caste-class polarity is a misplaced one. The idea of change from caste to class is a wrong perception. Caste as an ideology is a dangerous move and perhaps so is the case with 'the class alone' perspective as the basis of study of Indian society. However, no serious studies have been carried out by sociologists and other social scientists considering Indian society as a social formation vis-á-vis social stratification.

The Methodological Orientations

Indian sociologists and social anthropologists have not been quite sensitive to research methodology and field of study. Broadly speaking, they have been swept (barring a few exceptions) by currents of theory and method in the western countries. Even if it was not the case at an early phase of Indian sociology, a large number of sociologists followed the methods of study adopted by a few leading sociologists of that period. Thus, one could say that Indological approach, survey, participant observation and historical methods (or techniques) have dominated sociological research in India. A clear link between a method of study and a given theoretical perspective has generally remained vague in a large number of researches. Thus, the theoretical perspectives adopted by Indian sociologists have not remained rooted in Indian social reality. The methods of study have been unrelated to these perspectives. The methods have been adopted mainly due to two reasons: (a) the notion of scienticism has compelled a researcher to accept a particular method; and (b) convenience of accepting a method of study. We hardly find any study on social stratification which explains the correspondence between its theoretical perspective, method of study and data.

Beteille's study of caste, class and power in Sripuram village of Tanjore district in Tamil Nadu is based on intensive field-work (participant observation). Beteille writes: 'I did my field-work in Sripuram while living with people as one among them. I was permitted to live in the *agraharam* in a Brahmin house – a privilege, as I was often told, never before extended to an outsider and a non-Brahmin. I dined with the Brahmins and had access to most of their houses. I was perhaps the only non-Brahmin ever to have sat and eaten with the Brahmins in Sripuram on ceremonial occasions.

I was identified with the Brahmins by my dress, my appearance, and the fact that I lived in one of their houses.'[140]

Beteille admits that his identification with the Brahmins was not an unmixed blessing. The non-Brahmins and Adi-Dravidas took Beteille, like as one of the Brahmins of the village. Consequently, he could not elicit properly the required information about the non-Brahmins and the Adi-Dravidas. The reason for staying in *agraharam* as given by Beteille is: 'Had I lived with the non-Brahmins the Brahmins would not have moved freely with me. Had I lived with the Adi-Dravidas, the *agraharam* would have been unaccessible. I chose to live with the Brahmins for practical reason and also because this gave me an opportunity to gain some insight into the literate cultural tradition of the region.'[141]

Beteille admits certain limitations of his study. He writes: 'Had I lived with the Adi-Dravidas this study would perhaps have had a different focus.'[142] The other point is that 'the study is qualitative in its character and emphasis.'[143] The village has not been understood 'in quantitative and statistical terms.' Beteille says that he has understood the village's social life 'from within', 'in terms of the values and meanings attributed to it by the people themselves.'[144] It is mentioned by Beteille that his status as a resident of *agraharam* was curiously ambiguous one of 'outsider' as well as 'insider'. As Beteille claims, it gave him the advantage of both insider and outsider. Beteille writes: 'My field work was not done in a very planned or organized manner. I did not enter the field armed with a battery of hypotheses'.[145] Beteille feels that formulation of hypotheses 'would have done more harm than good'.[146] Beteille elsewhere that 'in adjusting oneself (Beteille himself) to a stratified community one learns much about the nature of stratification itself.'[147] The points raised in the article – 'The Tribulations of Field Work' by Beteille[148] are the same which he makes in his study of caste, class and power. Some observations given by P.N. Mukherji on participant observation in the form of criticism of Beteille's[149] view may be mentioned below.

Mukhreji formulates three questions: (a) By what criteria does the researcher select his community or small group for study? (b) Does the researcher enter the field first and then let the investigation take 'shape' or does he approach the field with a clearly formulated plan of investigation? (c) What indeed is the method of participant observation, and how are we to assess its utility in the Indian context?[150] Our interest is in the first two questions more than the third one. Simply, an interest to understand a community's social life cannot be the basis for an extensive study. Also some knowledge about the people cannot be the basis of an insightful investigation. The point is that some research objectives are always thought of beforehand. However, our concern is still more for the second question and we tend to agree with Mukherji's observation on that question. We, like Mukherji, do not agree with Beteille's statement that he went to Sripuram without a definite preference for any particular aspect of its social life; that he did not have an interest in the problem of social inequality. Beteille's assertion that he got interested in the study of social inequality after seeing the marks of stratification in virtually every sphere of life.[151] The danger in acceptance of Beteille's position is that it is not the cognitive understanding of society and explanations about society that determine our interests of research, but it is the observation of field that determines the object of study.

A number of questions could be raised about Beteille's method of study. Why did he not 'plan' his field work? Was his village a unique one? Did he not have any idea of a village in India? Did he not read Max Weber or Karl Marx before conducting the present study? Did he relate his data with the formulations of Weber in particular and of Marx and others in general after field work? Beteille perhaps knows about these questions on his study. There is no connection whatsoever between the 'battery of hypotheses' and 'concepts' which he has formulated, (may be after he completed his field work) and the method of study. Beteille's study lacks required *historical* perspective.

The formulations of Weber and Marx would demand a historical understanding of caste, class and power. Beteille has also ignored (perhaps unwittingly) the ideological implications of Max Weber's conceptual framework. The ghost of Marx was the basis of Weber's distinction between 'class, status and party.' Where was such a 'ghost' before Beteille? However, it is true that analysis of rituals and religion finds a negligent place in Beteille's study of Sripuram, but it is not clear whether it was consciously planned to chase the ghost of Louis Dumont's binary opposition of pure and impure or Srinivas' emphasis on the study of religion in Rampura. Certainly, Srinivas' impact on Beteille is seen in the advocacy of participant observation, but Beteille is unable to relate it with Weber's theory of social stratification and its implicit ideological moorings.

K.L. Sharma's study of the changing rural stratification system has been guided by 'a battery of hypotheses'.[152] Sharma expresses his concern for scarcity of multidimensional studies of rural social stratification. His study raises questions about 'caste' as an overarching stratification, about vertical or pyramidal arrangements of caste groups and caste (or group) as the unit of social ranking. Sharma questions the thesis of 'corporateness' about social ranking and social mobility. He uses both structural and cultural criteria in understanding of social stratification.

Emphasis on comparison based on variables such as economic conditions, geographical factors and cultural distinctiveness along with land-tenure systems is the hallmark of Sharma's study of social stratification in six villages of Rajasthan. The study is based on census and enumeration method, sampling, interview, case study, secondary data, and historical records, etc. Participant observation alone is not the stand of Sharma's study. Since the study was based on a well-thought of plan, these techniques were found useful for gathering a variety of information.[153] The study provides a 'mix' of qualitative and quantitative analysis of social stratification.

Anil Bhatt's complaint is that ethnographers and social anthropologists have made 'qualitative' studies of single villages or single or multiple castes and communities. They do not provide quantification, but have a tendency to generalize or typify their limited observations and studies. Generalization and quantification are closely related. A large part of Bhatt's study is based on quantitative data gathered through survey research and deals with macro-national and regional levels of social stratification. He talks of 'degrees' and 'amounts' instead of 'generally', 'approximately' and 'mostly', etc. in his analysis of data. Bhatt deals with individuals as members of a caste, caste as a group in relation to other castes, and the caste system as a dimension of social stratification in relation to socio-economic and political dimensions. Bhatt has collected large-scale data in more substantive and relevant context.[154] Bhatt writes: 'I have tried to be very explicit in relating the evidences to the theory'. Perhaps Bhatt has done more justice to Weber's conceptualization than Beteille, in regard to substantiation, unit of study and range of analysis.

There are a few village studies based on information collected by the use of questionnaire.[155] Computerization of data has also been reported in village studies. Techniques of scale analysis have been applied. In several studies, interview schedule has been used for data collection. However, most of the studies on social stratification in rural India are based on participant observation, interview and case study method. Studies of social stratification in urban India are based on survey method and questionnaire.

Let us now discuss briefly the Marxian method of study. The essence of this method is that the explanation comes from the conditions and structure of social reality. Marxian approach is a historical explanation. It takes into account the course of events over a period of time in a given society with regard to class relations among the people. It is an evolutionary approach. Some have called it emancipatory and hermeneutic in nature. For studying social stratification in the British period, A.R. Desai has analysed economy, agriculture, handicrafts, industries, means of transport, modern education, political and administrative set-up, class structure, the role of press, social and reform movements, etc. The perspective is dialectical-historical.[156] Historical data and studies were used relevant for this period of one hundred and fifty years. Bettelheim's study of caste and class structure in post-independence period uses the same approach. But between the two, Desai does more justice with Marxist approach and method of study.

The variants of the Marxist theory and method of study are found in the studies of D.P. Mukerji,[157] Kathleen Gough,[158] Gail Omvedt,[159] and Ramkrishna Mukherjee.[160] As we know that D.P.M. has analysed Indian tradition from the Marxist approach, but he collected a different sort of research material, compared with that of Desai and Bettelheim. He was more interested in understanding of the cognitive and meaning structures which formed the Indian tradition than the actual concrete classes. Gough and Omvedt consider caste as an important aspect of Indian society, and the study of caste along with class structure and mode of production is combined in their method. Gough has done this in her studies of South India,[161] and Omvedt has done this in her studies of Dalits in Maharashtra.[162] R.K.M has combined historical and census data with data relating to the present class and caste structure in his study of rural society in Bengal. Several other sociologists pursuing Marxist and non-Marxist dispositions have used historical method in their analyses of caste and class and agrarian movements.[163] Among the non-Marxist (or even anti-Marxist), Dumont is one who combines the method of Indology, abstracted empiricism and pseudo history in his well-known study – *Homo Hierarchicus.*[164]

The method of study largely determines the nature of data in a given study. As we know, a large number of studies on caste have used ethnographic accounts prepared by the British officers. Some have used scriptural texts as source of their analyses. Historical accounts and studies are found as data in few studies. However, in the post-independence period, generation of data by sociologists and anthropologists in both rural and urban areas has been a pronounced practice. This has been done through field studies based on techniques such as survey, interview, observation and case study.

The main problem is still to find out a proper connection between theory, method and data. Field studies with the use of research techniques such as survey, interview, observation and some statistical devices became so fashionable that researchers remained 'unarmed' or 'unaware' about the intrinsic connection between theory, method and data. In other words, the false notion of making a study scientific, simply by adopting these techniques of research has created innumerable problems. Secondly, the notion of 'science' in social sciences has been distorted by implementing it in such a vulgarized and unrealistic way. However, such a problem is seen more in the case of 'commercialization' of social research. It is this sociology of knowledge perspective which is lacking, that is, sensitization about nature of theory and its implications for method and data.

Notes

1. Max Weber, 'Class, status, party', in H.H. Gerth and C. Wright Mills (eds), *From Max Weber: Essays in Sociology,* London: Routledge & Kegan Paul Ltd., Paperback, 1970, pp. 180–195.
2. P.A. Sorokin, *Social and Cultural Mobility,* London: The Free Press of Glencoe, 1964.
3. Yogendra Singh, 'Sociology of social stratification', in *A Survey of Research in Sociology and Social Anthropology,* Vol. I (ICSSR), Bombay: Popular Prakashan, 1974, pp. 311–383.
4. Yogendra Singh, 'Sociology of social stratification in India-II', prepared for the *Second Survey of Research in Sociology and Social Anthropology* (ICSSR), New Delhi: 1981 (Mimeographed).
5. Yogendra Singh, op. cit., 1974, p. 311.
6. Ibid., p. 311.
7. Ibid., p. 312.
8. Cf. Y. Singh, Ibid., p. 313.
9. Ibid., p. 313. See also Raymond Aron's two definitions of class in Andre Beteille (ed.) *Social Inequality,* Penguin Books, 1969, pp. 67–68. The two definitions of class are: (i) the American in which the emphasis is on *nationalist* character, prestige and status- determined class, and (ii) the French, in which the *realist* tendency is there – class represents total reality, collective consciousness and class is different from stratum.
10. See, for example, Kingsley Davis and Wilbert E. Moore's 'Some principles of social stratification', *American Sociological Review,* Vol. 10, No. 2, 1945, pp. 242–249; and Talcott Parsons', 'An analytical approach to the theory of social stratification', and 'A revised analytical approach to the theory of social stratification', in Talcott Parsons', *Essays in Sociological Theory,* Glencoe, The Free Press, 1964. However, for the debate on the functional approach to social stratification, see Celia S. Heller (ed.) *Structured Social Inequality,* New York: The Macmillan Co., 1969.
11. Social classes are treated as concrete interacting groups in a given social situation. They are not treated as categories. The French sociologists and the Marxist social scientists have taken up this view.
12. Y. Singh, op. cit., 1974, p. 314.
13. Ibid., p. 314.
14. Ibid., pp. 311–382.

15. Y. Singh, op. cit., 1981.
16. Ibid., p. 1.
17. Ibid., p. 2.
18. See, R.S. Khare, '"Inside" approaches of "outside": some implications of a sociological debate', in Giri Raj Gupta (ed.) *Main Currents in Indian Sociology,* Vol. I, Delhi: Vikas Publishing House, 1976, pp. 20–58; S.C. Dube, 'Social sciences for the 1980s: from rhetoric to reality', *International Social Science Journal,* Vol. XXXIV, No. 3, 1982, pp. 495–502; and Y. Singh, 'The role of social sciences in India: a sociology of knowledge', *Sociological Bulletin.* Vol. 22, No. 1, 1973, pp. 14–28.
19. See Yogendra Singh, 'Role of social sciences in India: a sociology of knowledge', in S.C. Dube (ed.) *Social Science and Social Relations: Role of the Social Sciences in Contemporary India,* Simla, Indian Institute of Advanced Study, 1976; and K.L. Sharma, *Essays on Social Stratification,* Jaipur: Rawat Publications, 1980, pp. 1–25.
20. Iravati Karve, *Kinship Organisation in India,* Bombay: Asia Publishing House, 1958.
21. I.P. Desai, *Some Aspects of Family in Mahuwa,* Bombay: Asia Publishing House, 1964.
22. A.R. Desai, *Social Background of Indian Nationalism,* Bombay: Popular Book Depot, 1948.
23. The department of sociology at the University of Delhi came into existence in 1959 with Professor M.N. Srinivas as its Head. Professor Srinivas initiated studies in the areas of village community, family life, caste and kinship from the point of the British functionalism. However, the department of sociology at the University of Rajasthan which was established in 1961, had influence of American social science positivism as it was evident in its courses and researches. More or less similar orientation has been there in the case of the sociology department at Chandigarh.
24. Joan P. Mencher, 'The caste system upside down, or the not-so-mysterious east', *Current Anthropology,* Vol. 15, No. 4, 1974, pp. 469–493.
25. Satish Saberwal, 'Sociologists and inequality in India: the historical context', *Economic and Political Weekly,* Vol. XIV, Nos. 7 and 8, 1979, pp. 243–254.
26. K.L. Sharma, *Essays on Social Stratification,* op. cit., 1980 and 'Caste and class in India: some conceptual problems', A working paper, presented at the XVI All India Sociological Conference, 1982 (mimeographed).

27. C. Parvathamma, 'The remembered village: Brahminical odyssey.' *Contributions to Indian Sociology,* New Series, Vol. 12, No. 1, 1978, pp. 91–96.
28. Andre Beteille, 'Ideas and Interests: some conceptual problems in the study of social stratification in India', *International Social Science Journal,* Vol. 21, No. 7, 1969, p. 17.
29. Gunnar Myrdal, *Asian Drama: An Inquiry into the Poverty of Nations,* Vol. I, Penguin Books, 1968.
30. Mortan Klass, *Caste: The Emergence of the System in South Asia,* Philadelphia: The Institute for the Study of Human Issues, 1980.
31. S. Sinha, *Caste in India: Myth, Reality, Challenge,* New Delhi: B&R Publishing Company, 1982.
32. See, for example, E.R. Leach, 'Introduction: What should we mean by caste?' in E.R. Leach (ed.) *Aspects of Caste in South India, Ceylon and North-West Pakistan,* Cambridge: Cambridge University Press, 1960, pp. 1–10; M.N. Srinivas chooses to reply Leach's criticism of his concept of 'dominant caste' in 'Future of Indian caste', *Economic and Political Weekly,* Vol. XIV, Nos. 7 and 8, 1979, pp. 237–242, after a lapse of 19 years. See C. Parvathamma and R.K. Jain's criticisms of M.N. Srinivas in *Contributions to Indian Sociology,* op. cit., 1978; F.G. Bailey and A.K. Saran's criticisms of Louis Dumont's position on how to study Indian society are given in chapter 4 of this volume.
33. Y. Singh, op. cit., 1981, p. 10.
34. Ibid., pp. 9–10.
35. A.R. Desai, op. cit., 1948.
36. Celestin Bougiel, *Essays on the Caste System,* Cambridge: Cambridge University Press, 1971.
37. Louis Dumont, *Homo Hierarchicus,* London: Paladin, Granda Publishing Ltd., 1970.
38. A.M. Hocart, *Caste,* London: Mathew & Co., 1950.
39. Structural-functional orientation is predominantly found in village studies in the 1950s and 1960s. All the aspects of village life have been studied in terms of their interrelationships and village as a 'totality'. However, the British social anthropologists and sociologists have more in-depth studies than their American counterparts. Louis Dumont has been the pioneer of the structuralist perspective in regard to the study of caste system in India.
40. D. Thorner, in particular, has suggested the use of native concepts and categories for the study of agrarian stratification. D.P. Mukerji prefers to indigenization of Marxist approach for studying Indian

society. Some studies of agrarian structure and movements in particular have shown interest in historical-sociological analysis.

41. Studies on Hindu religion, urban setting, and class character of Indian state are illustrative of the concurrent interests in positivism, culturology and orthodox Marxism.
42. K.L. Sharma, *The Changing Rural Stratification System,* New Delhi: Orient Longman Ltd., 1974, p. 15.
43. These studies have highlighted *caste* as the most predominant institutional factor in Indian society. Some of them have analysed caste rank as the basis of social status, others have found it as an obstacle in economic development, as an interest group and as a basis of social solidarity and security.
44. Andre Beteille, *Caste, Class and Power,* Bombay, Oxford University Press, 1966, p. 4. See also Beteille's, 'Closed and open social stratification in India', *European Journal of Sociology,* Vol. 7, 1966, pp. 224–246.
45. Andre Beteille, 'Ideas and interests: some conceptual problems in the study of social stratification in India', op. cit., 1969.
46. Anil Bhatt, *Caste, Class and Politics,* Delhi: Manohar Book Service, 1975.
47. P.C. Aggarwal, *Caste, Religion and Power,* New Delhi: Shri Ram Centre for Industrial Relations, 1971.
48. K.E. Gough, 'Caste in a Tanjore village', in E.R. Leach (ed.), op. cit., 1960, pp. 11–60.
49. Ramkrishna Mukherjee, *The Dynamics of Rural Society,* Berlin: Akademie Verlag, 1957.
50. K.L. Sharma, op. cit., 1974, p. 24.
51. Y. Singh, op. cit., 1981, p. 10.
52. Ibid., p. 10.
53. Ibid., p. 11.
54. See M.N. Srinivas' concepts of Sanskritization and Westernization in his *Social Change in Modern India,* California: University of California Press, 1966.
55. See K.L. Sharma, *Essays on Social Stratification,* op. cit., 1980.
56. See Louis Dumont, op. cit., 1970; and M.N, Srinivas, Caste in Modern India and other Essays, Bombay: Asia Pub. House, 1970.
57. F.G. Bailey, 'Closed social stratification in India', *European Journal of Sociology,* Vol. IV; No. 1,1963.

58. Pauline Kolenda, *Caste in Contemporary India, Beyond Organic Solidarity,* California: Benjamin Cummings Publishing Company, 1978.
59. D.B. Miller, *From Hierarchy to Stratification,* Delhi: Oxford University Press, 1975.
60. Andre Beteille, *Caste, Class and Power,* op. cit., 1966.
61. Ibid., p. 3.
62. Ibid., p. 4–5.
63. Ibid., p. 12.
64. K.L. Sharma, op. cit., 1980, p. x.
65. P.C. Aggarwal, op. cit., 1971.
66. Anil Bhatt, op. cit., 1975.
67. Ibid., p. 1.
68. Ibid., pp. 1–4.
69. Ibid., p. 5.
70. Ibid., p. 5.
71. Characteristics of structural-functional studies have been mentioned earlier in this chapter.
72. Anil Bhatt, op. cit., 1975, p. 9.
73. Ibid., p. 9.
74. Victor S. D'Souza, *Social Structure of a Planned City Chandigarh,* New Delhi: Orient Longman Ltd., 1968.
75. Victor S. D'Souza, 'Caste and class: a reinterpretation', *Journal of Asian and African Studies,* Vol. 2, Nos. 3–4,1967.
76. Ibid., p. 48.
77. Rajni Kothari, *Politics in India,* New Delhi: Orient Longman, 1970.
78. Ibid., pp. 1–20.
79. Ibid., p. 10.
80. The emergence of the DMK and the ADMK in Tamil Nadu, the Telugu Desham in Andhra Pradesh, the Akali movement in Punjab and several 'sons-of-soil' movements in other parts of India have falsified the basic assumptions of Kothari's hypothesis about 'integration' politics in India.
81. Selig S. Harrison, *India: The Most Dangerous Decades,* Princeton, Princeton University Press, 1960.
82. Rajni Kothari, 'Introduction: Caste in Indian Politics', in Rajni Kothari (ed.) *Caste in Indian Politics,* New Delhi: Orient Longman Ltd., 1970.

83. Ibid., p. 4.
84. Ibid., p. 4.
85. Ibid., p. 5.
86. Ibid., p. 6.
87. Ibid., p. 8.
88. Ibid., p. 10.
89. Ibid., p. 11.
90. Ibid., p. 20.
91. F.G. Bailey, op. cit., 1957.
92. T.S. Epstein, *Economic Development and Social Change in South India,* Manchester: Manchester University Press, 1962.
93. F.G. Bailey, op. cit., 1957, p. 239.
94. C. Levi-Strauss, *The Elementary Structures of Kinship,* Oxford: Alden Press, 1969 (English edition).
95. L. Dumont, *Hierarchy and Marriage Alliance in South Indian Kinship,* Occasional Papers No. 12, London: Royal Anthropological Institute, 1957.
96. We have discussed in detail Dumont's view on how to study Indian society in the chapters 2 and 3.
97. See Y. Singh, op. cit., 1981.
98. L. Dumont, 'Caste: a phenomenon of social structure or an aspect of Indian culture?', in Anthony de Reuck and Julie Knight (eds), *Caste and Race: Comparative Approaches,* London: J&A Churchil Ltd., 1967, p. 33.
99. Ibid., pp. 33–35.
100. Harold A. Gould, 'Priest and contrapriest: a structural analysis of Jajmani relationships in the Hindu plains and the Nilgiri Hills', *Contribution to Indian Sociology* (NS), No. 1, 1967.
101. Veena Das, *Cognition and Reality,* Delhi: Oxford University Press, 1977.
102. Veena Das and J.P.S. Uberoi, 'The elementary structure of caste', *Contributions to Indian Sociology* (NS), No. 5, 1971.
103. E.R. Leach, '"Espirit" in Homo Hierarchicus', *Contributions to Indian Sociology* (NS), No. 5, 1971, p. 16.
104. T.N. Madan, 'On understanding caste', *Economic and Political Weekly,* Vol. VI, No. 34, 1971. *See* also T.N. Madan et al., 'On the nature of caste in India: a review symposium on Louis Dumont's Homo Hierarchicus', *Contributions ta Indian Sociology* (NS), No. 5, 1971, pp. 1–81.

105. Y. Singh, op. cit., 1981, p. 17.
106. Ibid., p. 18.
107. Mortan Klass, op. cit., 1980.
108. S. Sinha, op. cit., 1982.
109. See S.A. Dange, *India from Primitive Communism to Slavery,* Bombay: People's Publishing House, 1949; E.M.S. Namboodiripad, 'Caste conflicts vs. growing unity of popular democratic forces', *Economic and Political Weekly,* Vol. XIV, Nos. 7 and 8. 1979, pp. 329–336; and B.T. Ranadive, 'Caste, class and property relations', *Economic and Political Weekly,* Vol. XIV, Nos. 7 and 8, 1979, pp. 337–348.
110. Joan P. Mencher, op. cit., 1974.
111. M.S.A. Rao, *Social Movements and Social Transformation,* Delhi: Macmillan Co., 1979.
112. Rajendra Singh, 'Politicisation, protest and peasant movement in U.P.: a case study in the politics of land control in District Basti', in M.S.A. Rao (ed.). *Social Movements in India,* Delhi: Manohar Book Service, 1977.
113. P.N. Mukherji, 'Social movement and social change: towards a conceptual clarification and theoretical framework', *Sociological Bulletin,* Vol. 26, No. 1, 1977.
114. K.L. Sharma, op. cit., 1982.
115. S. Saberwal, op. cit., 1979.
116. S. Sivakumar and Chitra Sivakumar, 'Class and Jati at Asthapuram and Kanthapuram: some comments towards a structure of interests', *Economic and Political Weekly,* Vol. XIV, Nos. 7 and 8, 1979, pp. 263–286.
117. Y. Singh, op. cit., 1981, p. 24.
118. Ibid., p. 27.
119. Jaganath Pathy, 'Social stratification in an Orissa village', *Economic and Political Weekly,* Vol. X, June 7, 1975, pp. 893–901.
120. P.K. Bose, 'Agrarian structure, peasant society and social change: a study of selected regions in West Bengal', PhD thesis, JNU, New Delhi: 1979.
121. Hira Singh, 'Decline of feudalism: Marwar from 1870s to 1940s', PhD thesis, University of Delhi: 1981.
122. D.N. Dhanagare, 'Social origins of the peasant insurrection in Telengana', *Contributions to Indian Sociology* (NS), No. 8, 1974.
123. Dipankar Gupta, *The Shiva Sena Movement, 1966–1974: A Sociological Analysis,* PhD thesis, JNU, New Delhi: 1977.

124. K.E. Gough, 'Indian peasant uprisings', *Economic and Political Weekly,* Vol. IX, Nos. 32–34 (SN), pp. 1391–1412.
125. See a summary of the debate on the mode of production in Indian agriculture by Alice Thorner, 'Semi-Feudalism or capitalism: contemporary debate on classes and modes of production in India', *Economic and Political Weekly,* Vol. XVIII, Nos. 49, 50 and 51, 1982.
126. K.E. Gough, 'Colonial economics in south-east India', *Economic and Political Weekly,* Vol. VIII, No. 13, 1977, pp. 551–554. *See* also E.K. Gough, 'Modes of production in southern India', *Economic and Political Weekly,* Vol. XV, Nos. 5, 6 and 7, 1980, pp. 337–364.
127. See, Joan P. Mencher, op. cit., 1974; K.E. Gough, op. cit., 1977 and 1980; and A.R. Desai, op. cit., 1948; and *State and Society in India: Essays in Dissent,* Bombay: Popular Prakashan, 1975.
128. Charles Bettelheim, *India Independent,* London: Mac-Gibbon & Knee Ltd., 1968, p. 128.
129. Alice Thorner and Daniel Thorner, *Land and Labour in India,* Bombay: Asia Publishing House, 1974.
130. A.R. Desai, op. cit., 1975.
131. John Harris, *Capitalism and Peasant Farming,* Delhi: Oxford University Press, 1982.
132. Ibid., p. 9.
133. Ibid., p. 49.
134. Gail Omvedt (ed.), *Land, Caste and Politics in India,* Delhi: Authors Guild Publications, 1982.
135. Gail Omvedt, 'Caste, class and land in India: an introductory essay', in Gail Omvedt (ed.), op. cit., 1982, p. 13.
136. Ibid., p. 14.
137. Ibid., p. 14.
138. K.E. Gough, cf. Gail Omvedt, op. cit., 1982, p. 42.
139. K.L. Sharma, op. cit., 1982, p. 36.
140. Andre Beteille, *Caste, Class and Power,* op. cit., 1966, p. 9.
141. Ibid., p. 10.
142. Ibid., p. 10.
143. Ibid., p. 10.
144. Ibid., p. 10.
145. Ibid., pp. 10–11.
146. Ibid., p. 11.

147. Andre Beteille, 'The tribulations of field work', *Economic and Political Weekly,* Vol. VII, Nos. 31, 32 and 33 (SN), 1972, p. 1510.
148. Ibid.
149. Partha N. Mukherji, 'Some observations on participant observation', *Economic and Political Weekly,* Vol. VIII, No. 1, 1973, pp. 27–30.
150. Ibid., p. 27.
151. Andre Beteille, op. cit., 1972, p. 1510.
152. K.L. Sharma, op. cit., 1974, p. 24.
153. Ibid., pp. 22–27.
154. Anil Bhatt, op. cit., 1975, pp. 17–19.
155. P.C. Aggarwal, op. cit., 1971, p. 14.
156. A.R. Desai, op. cit., 1948.
157. D.P. Mukerji, *Diversities,* Delhi: People's Publishing House, 1958.
158. K.E. Gough, op cit., 1980.
159. Gail Omvedt, op. cit., 1982.
160. Ramkrishna Mukherjee, op. cit., 1957.
161. K.E. Gough, op, cit., 1977 and 1980.
162. Gail Omvedt, Cultural Revolt in a Colonial Society; The non-Brahmin. Movement in Western India, 1870–1930, *Pune: Scientific Socialist Education Trust, 1976.*
163. See for example, R. Singh, op. cit., 1977; K.L. Sharma, 'Jharkhand movement in Bihar', *Economic and Political Weekly,* Vol. XI, No. 2, 1976; and Satish Saberwal, op. cit., 1979.
164. Louis Dumont, op. cit., 1970.

CHAPTER 5

Village Studies

Theoretical and Methodological Orientations

Approaches for Studying Indian Society

Bernard C. Cohn identifies three major traditions of approach to Indian society at the end of the eighteenth century. These are: (a) the orientalist, (b) the administrative and (c) the missionary.[1] 'The orientalists seem to have been convinced that the texts were indeed accurate guides to the culture and society of the Hindus.'[2] The orientalist view implied that the Brahmins were the dominant group in the society. The Brahmins were seen as the centre of the social order – as the *prescribers* of norms- for all other Varnas, proclaiming their own superiority. It is said that 'the acceptance of a textual view of the society by the orientalists also led to a picture of Indian as being static, timeless and spaceless'.[3] Regional variation and hiatus between prescriptive-normative statements and the actual behaviour of individuals or groups were simply ignored by the orientalists. Village community was seen inferentially as a microcosm of Indian civilization. The missionaries' observations, however, raised several points about the nature of village community in India.

Cohn observes that the missionary view of India developed slightly later than the orientalist view.[4] Charles Grant called the people of India as a 'race of men lamentably degenerate and base' having 'a feeble sense of moral obligations', 'obstinate', 'malevolent' and 'licentious'. They had corrupt manners and 'vices'.[5] Grant's view about Indian society not only implied the social and cultural superiority of the British, but explicitly it meant condemnation and contempt of the people of India. Caste system, legal system, government and the despotic role of Brahmins were considered as the causes of the degraded state of the Hindus. The remedy lay in the elimination of Hinduism. The missionaries developed their view about Indian society on the basis of here say accounts and not so important and popular institutions. However, the missionary view paved a way for empirical investigations of Indian society and culture.

Both the missionaries and the orientalists were polar opposites in their assessment of Indian culture and society. However, they agreed that it was a society in which religious ideas and practices underlay all social structure. They accepted the supremacy of Brahmins and the Brahminical theory on the origin of the caste system. Both considered Hinduism as full of 'superstition' and 'abuses'. However, the orientalists admired the textual version of civilization and religion; the missionaries saw society and culture as 'corrupt' and 'pernicious'.[6] Both the approaches suffered from a lack of scientific objectivity and apriori conceptions about Indian society and culture. A knowledge of India's social, economic and political past and of the present became inevitable in view of these deficient views. Subsequently, it was also advocated that the caste system and the Hindu religion were not obstacles to economic and social development; obviously it was done so in the interest of the colonial rule in India.

The Provincial and Imperial Gazetteers of India and Census of India provided a systematic account of Indian society in the second half of the 19th century. The reports of revenue settlements also produced a great deal of material on the relation of people to the land and the organization of Indian rural society. Cohn is perhaps right when he states: 'The "official" view of caste was very much related to how the British collected information about the caste system.'[7] Most of the writings on caste system by the British administrators turned ethnographers have had the 'official' view before collecting relevant data. Census of 1901 recognized caste ranking based on 'social precedence' as expressed by the native people in a given region. These approaches were a pre-twentieth century phenomenon. Ethnographic studies of tribes, castes and villages became a pronounced practice in the early twentieth century. While concluding this important essay on the study of Indian society and culture, Cohn outlines the following features of the study of Indian society:

1. 'A broad-scale humanistically oriented tradition which emphasized the relationship between textual studies and a static model of contemporary Indian society;
2. an administrative tradition centred on the census for the study of caste which sought to see Indian society as a collection of discrete entities whose traditions and customs could be classified and studied;
3. a tradition of economic study which sought to describe the working of village economies, with some attention to the social structure of villages;
4. an anthropological tradition centred on the study of tribal peoples; and
5. an historical administrative strain which centred on the general theory of village organization in a broad comparative framework, but without an intensive ethnographic base.'[8]

All these points refer to the study of caste and village in India. The study of the Indian village began in the 18th century with the intensive survey work regarding landholdings. Later on, the Indian village was compared with the village in England. However, in the 20th century, intensive empirical studies of the economy of the villages became quite popular. The early systematic studies, particularly by Munro, Metcalfe, Maine and Baden-Powell considered the Indian village as a 'closed' and 'isolated' system. This view, however, created a lot of resentment among several anthropologists and sociologists. The studies of the Indian village in the 1950s were, therefore, based on the assumption that the Indian village was not 'static', 'isolated' and 'homogeneous'; it was changing; it had its connections with outside world, and it was highly differentiated.

Like the 'official view' of the caste system, the 'official view' of the Indian village was that India was a land of 'village republics', of self-sufficient and corporate villages. Dumont refers to three meanings of the term 'village community': (a) as a political society, (b) as a body of co-owners of the soil and (c) as the emblem of traditional economy and polity, 'a watch word of Indian patriotism'.[9] Thus, the village community in India has been seen as a part of India's polity and economy by scholars of differing dispositions such as Marx and Maine.

'A village is far from than a locale, more than just a collection of houses, lanes and fields'.[10] Mandlebaum points out that for a village it is a prime social reality. For the observer it is a principal unit for the understanding of the society. However, Dumont and Pocock do not accept the village either as a corporate group or as a useful unit of analysis.[11] It is true that these doubts are due to an exaggerated notion of the independence of an Indian village. There are multi-caste villages and also there are multi-village castes. The notion that Indian village is monolithic, atomistic and static is unacceptable to the students of village life in India. The Indian village has hardly been a 'republic', and a 'self-sufficient' unit. Village exogamy itself broke its isolation, atomism and independence. Its dependence on wider economic and political institutions and instrumentalities has been well brought out in the recent studies. Studies of village disputes have also revealed heterogeneity and diversity of interests among the people.

The British administrators as well as Indian national leaders preferred to call Indian village a 'republic', 'self-sufficient' and 'autonomous', due to their respective ideological and political predispositions. Village, even today, exists as a territorial cohesive unit. Village identity, solidarity and loyalty cut across caste and community, but divisive factors also exist, simultaneously. Land reforms, changes in power structure, and social and cultural mobility could be witnessed within a given village as well as in villages of a given area in terms of new form of stratificational relations.

Some Observations on Village Studies

It is noted that the 1950s and particularly the year 1955 marks a watershed in the studies of village communities. S.C. Dube's *Indian Village*, M.N. Srinivas' *India's Villages*, D.N. Majumdar's *Rural*

Profiles and McKim Marriott's *Village India* were all published in 1955.[12] These studies covered a vast range of data and experience from different parts of India. Village studies continued to be a central theme of sociological research in the 1960s and 1970s as well, but emphasis shifted from single-village holistic studies to multi-village comparative studies.[13] Diachrony was emphasized along with synchrony. Thus, historical materials were used along with intensive field data for analysing the changing rural society.[14] The 'folk-urban continuum' and 'little community' frameworks of Redfield were examined by B.R. Chauhan, D.N. Majumdar[15] and several others. Alternative to these dichotomies and continua were also suggested.[16] However, most of these suggestions were 'reactive' in nature rather than 'emanative' based on understanding of Indian social reality. Classifications of approaches are based on the nature of studies and not on the social reality which could be otherwise analysed independent of the approaches referred in the available studies. The point is that the cognitive and ontological bases of the studies themselves have been seriously questioned. Preference for one approach in relation to other does not offer a knowledge-view of social reality.

The questions are: Are these studies a result of the 'historicity' of Indian society, or a consequence of apriori acceptance of the approaches, methods and techniques of research? What are these approaches, methods and techniques? Where did they originate? How far the input of experience into these approaches and methods is different from the Indian situation? Is the social reality the same everywhere to facilitate the application of the same concepts and methods of study in all societies aud situations? Have the researchers taken care to eliminate or minimize the ideological biases inherent in the approaches and methods while applying them to the study of village community in India? These and several other questions bother us, and we shall reflect upon them here.

B.R. Chauhan in Rural Studies (a trend report) draws four lines of approach in the study of castes in relation to the village communities. These are: (a) one village and one caste, (b) one village and many castes, (c) one caste and many villages and (d) many castes and many villages.[17] The village studies are: (a) single village studies, (b) studies in two villages, and (c) multi-village studies.[18]

Chauhan does provide an exhaustive review of village studies, but he does not raise questions about their theoretical and methodological orientations. M.N. Srinivas, S.C. Dube, Yogesh Atal and Ramkrishna Mukherjee[19] have raised some important questions about village studies and their significance.

Srinivas observes that bias in favour of literary material is most clearly seen in the syllabi of Indological studies of Indian universities. 'Indology has come to be regarded as knowledge about India's past.'[20] Srinivas puts his position as follows: 'The only cure for this literary bias lies in doing field research. The field worker, confronted by the bewildering variety and complexity of facts as they actually are, is forced to relate what he sees to what he has assumed it to be, and the lack of correspondence between the two, results in his attempting to reassess the written material.'[21] Study of written (literary) and oral (folk) traditions has been undertaken with a comparative perspective by McKim Marriott.[22] However, emphasis on the study of 'tradition' is also found in the writings of D.P. Mukerji, S.C. Dube, M.N. Srinivas and Yogendra Singh.[23] These sociologists have differing perspectives on the study of tradition. We have discussed earlier this point in detail.

Srinivas states in the same essay: 'The point I am trying to make is that the observation of Hindu social life has been, and still is, vitiated by the *book-view* and the *upper-caste-view*. A sociological study of the Indian sociologists would yield interesting results' (emphasis added).[24] Dumont has been criticized for taking the 'book-view' of caste system, and Srinivas is said to have taken the 'upper-caste-view' of the village community. The criticisms of his concepts of 'sanskritization' and 'dominant caste' by Edmund Leach, C. Parvathamma and others are based on the upper-caste-view, which is attributed to have been taken in his study of the Coorgs.[25] A premium is given to empirical studies over the historical ones by Srinivas. He writes: 'Historical data are neither as accurate nor as rich and detailed as the data collected by field anthropologists, and the study of certain existing processes in the past.'[26] The method of intensive field study has been promoted by Srinivas not only through his study of Rampura, but a couple of students of Srinivas, namely, A.M. Shah, Andre Beteille and Anand Chakravarti,[27] have also carried out village studies by the method of intensive field-work.

Reacting with anger against the Indian economists in particular, Srinivas makes a strong plea for *participant observation* rather than survey method and statistical exercises. Srinivas writes about the researches done by the Indian economists: 'How could busy intellectuals afford to spend so much time among illiterate, ignorant and superstitious villagers?'[28] Sarcastically, Srinivas writes: 'Whatever data that were needed could be collected in short periods of time by young investigators, or presumably older ones who were not good enough to make a contribution to analysis.'[29] In continuation to the above statement, Srinivas writes: 'The net result of this view is the emergence of a helot class of full time data-gatherers who enable model-builders, theoreticians and other Brahmins to put forward their interpretations of the manner in which the economy functions.'[30]

There are a couple of points which we would like to make about Srinivas' view on social science. The object of study and nature of inquiry would normally determine the method of study. It would be wrong to say that intensive field-work is necessary for all sorts of village studies. Hard data about landholdings, occupation, caste structure, migration, population and education, etc. may demand survey (census and enumeration), whereas actual relations between higher and lower castes and classes, landowners, tenants and agricultural workers, and Jajmans and Kamias, etc. can be better understood by the method of intensive field-work. If the method of intensive field study is applied to all village studies irrespective of specific nature of data required, it would amount to methodological apriorism. No theory or method could be accepted as *academic cults,* as it has been done by scholars of 'orthodox' dispositions.

However, Srinivas' observations about the Indian economists are not quite unfounded. Economists in India today (including both Marxists and non-Marxists) are competing with each other in providing aggregate-data analyses with sophisticated models and statistical tests of reliability and validity. Their exercises have become increasingly unreadable and futile. They are more of 'mechanical' exercises. Srinivas therefore rightly observes: 'A completely instrumentalist view of social science seems to be axiomatic among economists if not amongst most social scientists in India. In fact, the few who are not convinced about the validity of this view, find themselves in a hopeless minority that they prefer silence at seminars, conferences and workshops.'[31] Alienation from grassroots reality, unfounded and fanciful assumptions about human behaviour are commonly found among the economists. Srinivas expresses his concern for divorce between field research and theory, and the division of labour between the theoretician-analyst and the fact-gatherer which have come about by survey researches.

A number of plus points of field-work are noted by Srinivas. It refers to a different set of approach, methods and techniques compared with macro-surveys. There is no difference in anthropological researches between the field-worker and analyst. A number of 'prescriptions' are given by Srinivas taking clues from Malinowski and Radcliffe-Brown. Srinivas ignores, however, the studies conducted by T.S. Epstein and F.G. Bailey which have bearing on the field-work, but have amply used historical and statistical materials, and have a comparative focus.[32]

There are other studies which have used census, archival and NSS data along with the field-work. The field-work has been used for studying networks and social mobility in India's urban centres.[33] Dasgupta undertakes an analysis of 126 village studies with two specific objectives: (a) to develop a simplified typology of village socio-economic systems based on a small set of key variables, and (b) to examine how far this typology helps to provide a dynamic theory of village job institutions under the given socio-political set-up in India.[34] Methodologically, it is a 'multivariate' approach. The studies included in the analysis have three features: (a) interdisciplinary approach, (b) extensive coverage of data, and (c) standard method of data collection based on a common research design.[35] Such a study and even a study of a single village based on the field-work or based on the combination of several methods and techniques would not be considered a useful exercise by Srinivas, if it did not study religion (pollution-purity), caste hierarchy and rules of marriage etc. Srinivas' field study has not gone beyond these themes of research and so is the case with many others. It is this perspective which limits the scope of sociological inquiry so far as the protagonists of the tradition of the field-work are concerned.

S.C. Dube prepares willy-nilly a case for the application of structural-functional approach for studying the Indian village community.[36] He refers to three criticisms of the intensive field studies: (a) these do not provide diagnostic or even illustrative case studies for understanding structure and process; (b) village is viewed as a *biotic* community, and not as a synthesized community; and (c) these studies lack a coherent frame of reference relevant to the structure and organization of Indian society.[37] Let us quote from Dube to substantiate his preference for the structural-functional approach. 'The concepts of great and little traditions, sanskritization, and universalization and parochialization offer us a good starting point.'[38] 'The structural-functional and themal approaches provide us with more or less satisfactory conceptual tools for the study of village communities.'[39] 'Redfield's folk-urban continuum provides one such conceptual framework.'[40]

However, Dube cautions us about the operational contradictions and difficulties. Dube suggests that contextual, classical and local traditions as well as the regional (culture-area), western (ideological-technological) and emergent national (nativistic-reinterpretational-adaptive) traditions may be useful to the study of the Indian village community.[41] This is put forth as an alternative to Redfield-Marriott-Srinivas' schema of studying Indian village community. But Dube's fascination for structural-functional approach remains intact. He writes: 'A good study of change invariably follows a good structural- functional themal study of a society, and together these need sustained work by trained social scientists.'[42] Yogesh Atal touches more upon the viability of Indian village as a unit of study.[43] He also suggests hypotheses for determining the representativeness of the Indian village.[44]

A.R. Desai rightly observes that Ramkrishna Mukherjee's approach to the study of rural society is qualitatively different from that of Srinivas, Dube and Atal.[45] Mukherjee analyses colonial forces and factors which led to the study of villages.[46] He compares and contrasts village studies conducted by social anthropologists, sociologists and economists, and points out that the economists have ignored the socio-cultural matrix of the village community, whereas the sociologists and anthropologists have ignored the economic and class matrix in their village studies. Mukherjee prefers a combined or synthesized approach which can account for sociocultural as well as economic aspects of village life. Mukherjee's well-known book – *Dynamics of a Rural Society*[47] provides a very useful analysis of caste (sociocultural) and class (economic) relations and hierarchy. Methodologically too, it combines historical as well as empirical data.

Village Studies in the 1950s

The volumes – *Village India: Studies in the Little Community*[48] edited by McKim Marriott and *India's Villages*[49] edited by M.N. Srinivas are the most well-known collections of village studies published in the 1950s, and even today they could be considered eminently relevant. Louis Dumont and D.F. Pocock wrote a long review article in the first issue of their journal – *Contributions to Indian Sociology* on these two sets of village studies.[50] It would be in the fitness of things, if the issues raised by the editors and contributors of these two volumes are stated before we take up the views expressed by Dumont and Pocock and some others on these studies on *Village India*. Let us first take the main points discussed in McKim Marriott's – *Village India*.

Robert Redfield and Milton Singer in 'Foreword' state that 'the view of Indian civilization' is taken in the volume *Village India*.[51] It consists of studies of eight villages. The studies are not a representative sample. But they provide 'a grass-roots view', that is, more nearly representative of India today than any single account would be. This could be claimed about Srinivas' *India's Villages* as well. Mandelbaum provides a comparison of the eight villages in his paper in the present volume,[52] including relative isolation and relative dependence of these villages. Redfield and Singer state the objective of the volume under discussion as follows: 'Indeed, the primary interest that brought about this volume is not the effort to understand India and her changes. It is the effort to understand how to seek understanding of any great civilization and its enormously complex changes through anthropological studies of villages.'[53] Questions of 'method' came up very sharply in the seminar of which the present volume is an outcome. These questions are as follows:

1. 'What forms of thought for understanding a small community are relevant when the community is an Indian village?
2. What changes in ways to which anthropologists are accustomed when they work in isolated tribal communities are demanded, when they work in a village that is part of a village society, when they study a local culture that is part and cause and product of an ancient civilization?'[54]

Further, the two anthropologists say that the question is not 'what does this (the present volume) say about India?' The question is: 'What does this say about the interests and way of work of the anthropologist who wrote this paper: what did he try to find out and how did he go about?'[55] Thus, the present volume poses theoretical as well as methodological issues on the study of Indian village. Two very pertinent questions are asked by Gough: (a) 'To what extent is Kumbapettai an isolable social unit?' (b) 'And to what extent it is changing in this respect?'[56] Gough analyses economic organization, local administration, ritual practices at the village level, intercaste relations (of a social nature) within the village, and some general relations of the village to the wider community.

Srinivas states that he spent *twelve months* (emphasis added) doing field-work in Rampura.[57] The account given by Srinivas gives the impression that Rampura was an 'isolate'. He analyses several aspects of social organization of village, including religious, ritual and hierarchical. However, he refers to competition also, but all this is within the social organization of the village. Village solidarity, interdependence among castes, patron-client relations, rule of a dominant caste and a counterbalance of village unity and caste unity are some of the important aspects studied by Srinivas, which clearly show his acceptance of 'functional approach' to the study of Indian village. Gough on the other hand shows that the village she has studied is undergoing radical change. Disintegration and growing interdependence on urban or national institutions are clearly visible. She talks of the decline of the economic and social power of Brahmins and rise of the depressed sections of the village community.[58]

Gough's approach and method of study are evident in the following statement: 'It is clear that, in general, the social structure of the Tanjore village is changing from a relatively closed stationary system, with a feudal economy and cooperation between ranked castes in a way ordained by religious law, to a relatively "open", changing system, governed by secular law, with an expanding capitalist economy and competition between castes which is sometimes reinforced and sometimes obscured by the new struggle between economic classes.'[59] She observes that the village will not any longer be a useful isolate for study. Economic relations in the village even today are affected by broader government policies and economy. Thus, Gough adopts a 'class-view' of the Indian village, whereas Srinivas has a 'culture-view'. Gough's study is diachronic, and Srinivas' is synchronic.

Cohn looks at the caste relations in the village from the viewpoint of the Chamars (a depressed caste).[60] It is not a class-view of caste as seen in the case of Gough, but certainly Cohn's analysis is diachronic, and he also analyses factors external to the village, which brought about changes in intercaste relations. Beals analyses the factors external to the village, which account for the transformations that have taken in it.[61] Gough, Cohn and Beals conducted intensive studies of their respective villages for about a period of twelve months. Gitel P. Steed also did a twelve months research in a Hindu village in Gujarat, but her approach is both *sociological and ontogenetic*.[62] Village social structure and its components and psychological techniques are interposed in Steed's study of 'personality formation'. She analyses what she calls 'socio-logical horizons of personality formation',[63] which include the impact of the legal system, the land reforms, rulers and subjects, the greater Rajput tradition and seniority and authority among the rulers.[64] Class structure and caste and kinship as the most insular traditions are also analysed as the factors affecting the personality formation.

It would be quite useful to mention a few methodological points about Oscar Lewis' comparative analysis of peasant culture in India and Mexico.[65] Lewis writes: 'This study represents one of the relatively few examples of firsthand comparative field research by the same investigator in peasant society in the different parts of the world.'[66] The traditional library methods would not be of much help for such a study. A common frame of reference, similar methods of work, and a similar sense of problem are some of its distinctive advantages. About the question of the degree to which it is a part, Oscar Lewis observes: 'It is my own belief that almost any village in a predominantly agricultural nation reflects some distinctive aspects of the nation, its culture, and its problems.'[67] Lewis hopes that his comparative study of the Mexican and the Indian villages would show differences not only between the two villages, but also between the two countries.

Lewis gives a fairly detailed account of similarities and contrasts between the two villages. He concludes: 'Neither Tepoztlan nor Rani Khera is an isolated entity. Each in its own distinctive way is part of a larger socio-cultural system, a larger whole – the region and the nation – through which it must be understood.'[68] Anthropological studies in Mexico have been characterized by an *ideological localism,* whereby each little community is treated as self-sufficient and isolated.[69] Further, Lewis writes: 'In studying communities in Mexico (or India) it is important that the anthropologist becomes a student not merely of the single community but of the region and the nation as well. The anthropologist must be sufficiently versed in the more important historical, geographical, economic, and cultural characteristics of the region and nation to be able to place his community in relation to each of them, and to indicate just what the community is representative of in the larger sense ... the anthropologist must know what is unique to his community and what it shares with broad areas, what is new and what is old, what is primitive and what is modern.'[70]

Questions about the village as a community are also raised by Lewis. These are: (a) 'Is the village a community?' (b) 'To what extent do the physical limits of the village define the limits for these dimensions?' (c) 'Or to what extent do these aspects of community spill over into other villages so that the community might better be defined in terms of units larger than the single village?' (d) 'What is quality of social relations, of mutual interdependence of persons or social groups within each village?'[71]

The answers to these questions smack of academic superiority of Western social science models, approaches and methodologies. Lewis studies, in fact, the Indian village from the point of Mexican village. Some of the conclusions drawn by him speak of this bias in his study. He quotes from his study of the Mexican village and argues that it applies to the Indian village as well. He fails to recognize the historicity of the Indian village, its economy, social organization and polity, etc. while adopting the anthropology of Tepoztlan to Rani Khera. The *ideological localism* of the two villages cannot be the same, however Lewis treats the two villages theoretically and methodologically at the same plane and yet he establishes superiority of the Mexican village at the structural level. The following statements could be cited:

1. 'From an economic point of view, the village of Rani Khera is a more clearly isolable and self-contained community than the village of Tepoztlan.'[72]
2. 'From the point of view of village government Tepoztlan stands out as a more clearly organized and centralized community.'[73]
3. 'Village-wide leadership in Tepoztlan is formally expressed by the local government. In Rani Khera it does not yet exist.... As yet, there are no village heroes or outstanding citizens who are popular for their contribution to village welfare as a whole.'[74]
4. 'In Rani Khera, leadership is limited to faction leadership and is primarily of a protective and defensive nature in which each faction or combination of factions defends its family interests.'[75]
5. 'In Tepoztlan there is more verbalization about village community spirit.'[76]

'Stability' of Rani Khera is immensely highlighted, whereas dynamism of Tepoztlan is overstated. This is evident from the above statements. It is our impression that everything is well-in-order in the Mexican village, whereas everything is in archaic form in the Indian counterpart. This point is further substantiated in another comparison between the two villages. 'In the case of Tepoztlan, trade is primary, religious pilgrimages take second rank, and kinship occupies a very low third. In the case of Rani-Khera, kinship is primary, religious pilgrimages rank a low second and trade a very low third.'[77] Further, 'In so far as the role of kinship is concerned, India is much more primitive (or tribal) than Mexico and represents a different stage of socio-cultural evolution'.[78]

The missionaries in the 18th and 19th centuries made similar observations about Indian society asserting their superiority as a 'race' over the 'primitives' of India. Redfield's notion of 'little community' is fully justified by Oscar Lewis in studying Indian society with the pretensions of calling it a 'peasant society', like that of Mexico. A simple fact that kinship is more than a system of affinal and consanguineal relations, is forgotten by Lewis. Kinship is not only a principle of social organization in a cultural sense, but it is also a system of property relations, allocation of rights and duties and also of division, bifurcation and dissensions. To consider it simply an archaic element of Indian society would be far from reality.

In a very well-argued essay, 'Little Communities in an Indigenous Civilization', McKim Marriott discusses the small world of a village within the universe of Indian civilization. He also asks two questions: (a) Can such a village be satisfactorily comprehended and conceived as a whole in itself? (b) Can understanding of one such village contribute to understanding of the greater culture and society in which the village is imbedded? To provide answers to these questions, Marriott discusses certain aspects of social structure and religious culture of Kishan Garhi,[79] the village studied by him in north India. The paradox is that if 'yes' is given in the case of the first question, then 'no' is given in regard to the second. Thus, there is an inverse relationship between the two questions. Marriott explains this problem as follows: 'We cannot say both that an Indian village is comparable with a primitive isolate and also that it is dependent upon and part of a system that is outside itself. We cannot claim simultaneously that the great tradition of Indian civilization is relevant and that it is irrelevant to the understanding of peasant life.'[80]

Kishan Garhi is not like an isolated whole, a world in itself. It has internal divisions of economic interest groups. It grows crops which are sold outside the village. There are many external economic relationships. Internal divisions are also in matters of marriage and kinship. The village is divided politically too in terms of factions. Marriott observes: 'These structural facts make Kishan Garhi seem very much less than an isolated whole in the primitive sense.'[81] However, Kishan Garhi is 'isolable'. Marriott writes: 'But still I am compelled to go on to say that the village of Kishan Garhi is like a living thing, has a definable structure, is conceptually a vivid entity, is a system – even if it is one of many subsystems within the larger socio-politico-religio-economic system in which it exists. Especially am I so compelled if I look at the concerns and emphases that the people of the village express, and if I try to evaluate the structural aspects of their lives as they evaluate them.'[82] Marriott relies on certain cultural practices, norms and etiquettes, etc. for considering Kishan Garhi as an 'isolate'. The question are: How far these notions and practices are the core of the village life? Are they not peripheral aspects of social structure? To us, Marriott's phenomenological anthropology looks somewhat superficial as a methodological device.

Marriott writes: 'In India we are on middle ground'.[83] The village reaches beyond its central locus far into the outside world, and the outside world in turn reaches into the most central core of the village society. The following observation of Marriott may be referred here: 'Although Kishan Garhi is a conservative and a relatively traditional village, I cannot say it is a self-contained, complete little community comparable with primitive little communities. Nor, on the other hand, can I doubt that it is a community, and a clearly isolable community for its residents. So how am I to conceive it within its larger universe?'[84] Marriott accepts the notions of 'levels of socio-cultural integration', 'active fields', 'the folk-urban continuum' and 'levels of communal relations'[85] for analysing relations between 'primary civilization' and 'secondary civilization'. An indigenous great tradition remains in constant communication with its own little traditions. The processes of 'universalization' and 'parochialization' facilitate interaction between the great and little traditions. Besides the role of state and caste, Marriott has analysed festivals and deities in great detail with a view to understand the nature of the village community in India.

The volume *Village India*, edited by Marriott, consists of eight studies from the states of Karnataka, Tamil Nadu, Uttar Pradesh and Gujarat, whereas *India's Villages*,[86] edited by Srinivas, includes fifteen studies from the states of Karnataka, Rajasthan, Kerala, Himachal Pradesh, Tamil Nadu, Uttar Pradesh, Odisha, Punjab, Bengal and Andhra Pradesh. Four authors are common to these volumes. Papers included in *India's Villages* were earlier published in *Economic Weekly* (later on renamed in 1965 as *Economic and Political Weekly*). The papers in Srinivas' volume have been just picked up, whereas Marriott's volume includes papers which were prepared for a seminar. Theoretical and methodological issues have been carefully taken up by the contributors to the *Village India*. However, such a focus is not seen in the *India's Villages*.

The main issues are, however, the same in both the studies. The unity of the village, the solidarity of caste, extensions of the village into the outside world and the interpenetration of the wider world into the village, kinship networks, affinal ties, village exogamy, extensions of village economy and the role of outside economy on village have been listed and discussed by all the contributors.[87] A lack of thematic unity in the two volumes is also noted by Dumont and Pocock as they observe that the essays are 'tentative' and 'unrelated to each other'.[88] Dumont and Pocock have mainly reviewed the papers published in Marriott's *Village India*. Let us understand what they have commented on these two studies.

L. Dumont and D.F. Pocock's View on Village Studies

Dumont and Pocock have raised two questions which we have already stated earlier in this chapter. (a) 'Is the village indeed the social fact which it has for so long been assumed to be? (b) Is it possible or profitable to compare villages as such or should we not rather most profit by this mass of information by considering it from another point of view?'[89] Dumont and Pocock compare *Village India* and *African Political Systems* to have a comparative view. They observe that the two volumes (edited by Srinivas and Marriott) differed in their emphases, but had a common view of their objects and of their methods.[90] The contributors to *Village India* share little in the way of common assumptions. The Foreword by the general editors does not set out to do more than summarize the contents and discuss then the most general point of view. The articles have then, for the most part, the value and the weaknesses of initial reports.[91] The other observations are as follows:

The sociology of India has only properly begun in the ten years despite long period of Anglo-Indian contact.[92] Obviously, the editors of *Contributions to Indian Sociology* do not consider the pre-1947 sociology in India as sociology proper. We have discussed this point in the second chapter that sociology in India emerged in the second half of the 19th century and in the first half of the 20th century, independent of influences of the British and the American sociologies. It is obvious that what Dumont and Pocock consider as sociology emerged in India in the 1950s. Thus, they intend to import cultural and academic imperialism of the West, particularly through structuralist and field-work approaches of the French and the British anthropologists, respectively. Studies of African societies are a guide for Dumont and Pocock to analyse the state of sociology in India. They fall prey to theoretical and methodological apriorism and at the same time advocate 'a sociology for India', different from sociologies of other countries and continents.

The field worker in England approaches his field with questions of a historical or social nature and is concerned with the *social wholes in themselves,* to describe and analyse their present functioning. The entire debate whether Indian village is an 'isolate' or not – has emanated from this knowledge of the British social anthropology. Whether field-work of the sort done by British anthropologists would be the best method to study or not is a pertinent question. The viewpoint whether we analyse and understand the past or only the present of India's villages has also come from the same source. All the contributors to *Village India* as well as to *India's Villages* consider Indian village 'isolable', study its present and through the field-work approach, hence historicity of India's villages is forgotten. Dumont and Pocock seem to support the 'imperialist' view about Indian sociology. They write: '... Indian sociology cannot only profit itself at the present time by becoming aware of its distinctive problems and methods but can also profit social anthropology in general and in the future. Above all, the Indian sociologist has to become conscious of the suppositions which he takes over from more advanced studies and to progress by adopting them to his particular field.'[93]

Obviously, comparison of Indian village is made with the African tribes. The methods of study and conclusions of the studies of African tribes are applied to the Indian villages. The questions referred above have originated in regard to those tribes and have been applied to the Indian situation. Dumont and Pocock's view that Indian society is 'unique', and consequently Indian sociology too would be 'unique', is evident in their statement regarding interaction between *a general idea and the local working out of that idea.*[94] They write: 'If we wish to understand the situation of a Brahmin in a particular village we must know what the Brahmin stands for in Indian civilization and reciprocally our understanding of the latter will be enriched by our local study. It seems to us that there is no question of *either-or* here, but of both. This interaction is a social fact of Indian society and must be reflected in the mind of each investigator.'[95]

Dumont and Pocock pose the main problem of *Village India* as follows: 'How relevant are holistic methods of analysis for studies of villages in India? And if such studies make use of such holistic methods of analysis, then what relevance do these studies have for understanding problems which concern all of India?'[96] Thus, the problem is of the relevance of studying the microcosm. How far the village is representative of Indian civilization? Is India made up of villages alone? Is there microcosm-macrocosm opposition? Dumont and Pocock respond to these questions as follows:

'There is an obsession with defining the *unit* of study as if this were the prior requisite to an analysis of the society; a confusion, that is to say, between the necessary delimitation of a field of enquiry with the result of that enquiry. A field-worker takes a village as a convenient centre for his investigations and all too easily comes to confer upon that village a kind of sociological reality which in fact it does not possess. The architectural and demographic fact which the village is, lures us away from a structural perspective, where things exist only in the relations which are the proper objects of study, to an atomistic or elemental point of view where things exist in themselves.'[97] Caste and kinship are the referents and not the whole of the village, and therefore, caste as it is found in Indian society should be seen in a given village. It is the caste and kinship that link the people of one village with that of others. Apriorism is implicit when village is taken as a 'whole', also apriorism is there in the 'caste view' of village and in the study of caste itself independent of village. Dumont is perhaps aware of these limitations of his perspective and still he prefers to advocate this for studying Indian village community.

Finally, Dumont and Pocock quote from the 'Foreword' of *Village India*. 'What does this say about India? What does this say about the interests and way of work of the anthropologist who wrote this paper? What did he try to find out and how did he go about it?'[98] The answer to these questions by Dumont and Pocock is: 'Such questions are valid and yet if the suggestion is that interest is separate from method and both are undetermined by the material to be studied, we cannot agree. For us it seems most necessary at the present time to assert first of all that the sociological perspective is distinct and as objective in India as elsewhere, and secondly that the nature of Indian society involves certain shifts and adjustments of that perspective which, in turn will profit the science of sociology as a whole.'[99]

As mentioned earlier, we may again restate that according to Dumont, the 'village community' has three meanings: (a) as primarily a political society; (b) as a body of co-owners of the soil; and (c) as the emblem of traditional economy and polity.[100] The first refers to the village Panchayat and the second refers to the land tenures. However, the third is not analysed by Dumont due to lack of sufficient historical material. *Caste and kingship* are considered as the main features by Dumont in the analysis of village community,[101] which, according to him, have been ignored by Maine in *Village Communities in the East and West*.[102] We have already given a description of Dumont's view, and our aim is not to provide here a history of studies on the village community.

Structural Analysis of the Village Community in India

Let us now refer to S.C. Dube's *Indian Village*, which was also published in the year 1955.[103] Dube does not take a position different from Marriott and some other scholars. He recognizes 'semi-autonomous character' of the Indian village, yet does not regard it as 'static, timeless and changeless.'[104] Dube provides a classification based on certain criteria.[105] He writes: '... It is difficult to regard any one village as typical or representative of rural India as a whole.'[106] It cannot be representative of its 'culture area'. Dube's study of Shamirpet provides descriptions of social, economic and ritual structure, family ties, levels of living and living together. It is no doubt a descriptive study of the village community, but the understanding one gets is that the village is under a multiplicity of influences. Family, caste and village council are transforming their traditional character.[107] We get the impression that the change has been for the good of the village people.

D.N. Majumdar's study – *Caste and Communication in an Indian Village*,[108] and Oscar Lewis's study – *Village Life in Northern India*,[109] have emphasised on 'de-sanskritization', 'horizontal mobility', and role of caste and clan in factionalism, respectively. These studies are not different in their theoretical and methodological orientations from that of S.C. Dube and other studies. However, the studies by Bailey, Epstein, Beteille, Gough, Ishwaran, Mukherjee, Rao and Sharma[110] have emphasized on specific aspects of the village community, such as social change, economic development, social stratification, class relations, economy, overlap between caste and class, urbanization, etc. However, it is not to say that such studies have replaced the holistic, monographic studies of the village community of the 1950s.

On the lines of Srinivas, Marriott and Majumdar, another edited volume under the caption – *Change and Continuity in India's Villages* was brought out by K. Ishwaran at the beginning of the 1970s.[111] The village studies are from the States of Himachal Pradesh, Karnataka, Uttar Pradesh, Kerala, Tamil Nadu, Maharashtra and Andhra Pradesh. However, compared to the earlier studies, the studies included in this volume are qualitatively different in terms of both theoretical and methodological orientations. The shift is clearly visible. Ishwaran observes that the changes in the village society are *national-oriented* and *global-oriented*.[112] Not only challenges have come from outside, but institutional mechanisms have also developed from within both, as a response to the challenges and as a device to meet the new demands of the village community.

Ishwaran writes: 'These (village) studies have generally established the need for two approaches: first, the need for analysing social change in the terms of multiple factors rather than in terms of any single factor; second, the need to correlate micro-anthropological studies with macro-sociological analyses. On the one hand we need intensive field studies of village life, but on the other hand, we also need to link up such studies in order to map the morphology and content of social change in wider terms.'[113]

It is said that the methodological and conceptual framework of British structural-functionalism provided a somewhat lopsided picture of the Indian village with emphasis on structural continuity rather than structural change. Apriori Indological perspectives have been prominent in such studies. We would go along with Ishwaran and say that land-tenure systems, modern education, legal system and technological devices have been almost ignored as factors of change in the British as well as the post-British periods. Most of the contributors to this edited volume have not found much of explanatory power in the culturological concepts, such as sanskritization and westernization. Social change today has created new structural dilemmas; these are different from the old ones. Y. Singh, therefore, refers to the concept of 'levels' for analysing social change.[114]

Multidimensionality of concepts, approaches and aspects of study is the message of the essays by Berreman, Mencher, Beals, Elder, Gough and Singh.[115] Let us quote Gough to highlight the 'shift' in the village studies. 'The value of studies of change in local communities is that they illustrate some of the local details involved in the broad sweeps of change occurring in the total society. The community studies are not very illuminating unless made within the framework of knowledge and theory about what is happening to the larger society – in this case, to Kerala, beyond that to India, and beyond that still to the relations between former colonies and both new and old power centres in the Western and Communist worlds. Understanding of the wider society in turn requires a grasp of its main structural features in successive periods.'[116] Gough undertakes a historical analysis and collates it with field-work. Similar exercise is undertaken by Mencher in her study of a village in Tamil Nadu.[117] Ishwaran says that the following questions have been discussed in the contributions to the volume edited by him:

1. What is the nature of social change?
2. What areas of village are undergoing change?
3. What is the content and goal of such change?
4. What are the channels of social change?
5. What are the intrinsic and extrinsic sources of social change?
6. What are the prospects for future change?[118]

Let us also admit that all the studies emphasize on structure and change, history and empiricism and on both non-Marxist and Marxist categories of analysis. All of them have found culturological concepts and categories inadequate for understanding the Indian village community. They see the village community neither as an 'isolate' nor as 'isolable'. The Indian village is a part of social formation at various levels, such as state, nation and even global.

We wish to give an illustration of an another trend in the village studies. The volume – *Pills Against Poverty* by Goran Djurfeldt and Staffan Lindberg[119] is a problem-specific study of a village. The same authors have published another book entitled – *Behind Poverty: The Social Formation in a Tamil Village*. We shall refer to the first study just to illustrate our main contention. This study examines health and health policies in a Tamil village. The study reveals that it is wrong to treat the health situation as a natural product; it is rather a historical and social one. What is labelled as 'tropical diseases' could equally well be labelled as 'Diseases of the Poor'. Thus, health problems are related to economic and social processes, they are not *technical* in nature; they are in fact political and economic ones.[120] The strategy of the field study was as follows:

1. an extensive census covering demographic and economic subjects;
2. an ethnographic data collection through unstructured interview, specialist interviews, case-studies, small sample studies, and participant observation; and
3. a conventional sociological sample survey of 200 households.[121]

The theoretical orientation of the above study is self- evident in the questions asked relating to disease as a social phenomenon and the survival of the indigenous medicine. The modern Western system of medicine is a bourgeois production - a part of capitalist exploitation. Medical research itself is regulated and controlled by bourgeois interests. 'The dominant medical ideology today defines health problems as technical problems, rather than as political ones.'[122] Health is socially defined, and a socially produced natural reality. Both infrastructure and superstructure (political) have determined the social reality of disease.[123] This study, in fact, also proposes a revision of orthodox Marxism by taking into account the superstructural determination of health practices and health cure.

In a collection of village studies the often repeated issues of village, as a unit of study, the sociological reality of a village, village as an isolated unit, village patriotism/conflicts, relevance of univillage studies, 'one-man' depth studies, etc. have been discussed by Biplab Dasgupta.[124] Dasgupta classifies village studies into (a) fact-finding empirical studies, and (b) problem- oriented studies.[125] In the first category, the studies in the 1950s were conducted on a large scale. The studies of the second type were taken up in the 1960s and 1970s with different theoretical perspectives. Dasgupta shows his preference for the second type of studies. He says that the in-depth village studies have three major shortcomings, particularly in view of Srinivas' emphasis on the use of participant observation in village studies. According to Dasgupta, subjective assessment of the individual researcher, highly expensive in proportion to output, and unrepresentative of the rural population are the three major limitations.[126] Intra-village studies with comparable variables and units would be more relevant than 'holistic' studies.

Survey, census perspective of village studies, farm management surveys, NSS view of village studies, resurveys, etc. have been discussed in this collection as a substitute as well as a supplement to the in-depth studies. It is clear from the studies and views reported in this volume and the one edited by K. Ishwaran that the enthusiasm for conducting 'holistic' studies with emphasis on culturological orientation has considerably dwindled in the

1960s and the 1970s. Emphasis is now on structural analysis of specific issues and problems of the village life.

G. Parthasarathy examines the state of 'the village poor' in the Indian village studies.[127] He asks how much these studies tell us about 'class-relations', relations between the rich and the poor, the dominant and the weak and about the forces of change. What is that they tell us about the policies of government and their relevance/irrelevance for the poor. He asks the question: 'What are the insights that village studies offer in respect of the observed impact?'[128] Some people have dismissed village studies as 'cow-dung economics',[129] but Parthasarathy feels that they provide useful insights into the problems of the village poor. A study of the dynamics of the system within which the poor grow and multiply should be undertaken with a multidisciplinary effort.[130]

Concluding Remarks

Let us conclude by saying that we have touched upon the major theoretical orientations in the village studies, namely, structural-functional, structuralist and structural-historical (both Marxist and non-Marxist). We have also dealt with the often debated point – village as a unit of study. Our view is that this has originated from the Western scholars who have/had a certain view of the tribes which they studied or knew before they studied the Indian village community. Robert Redfield's concepts of little community, peasant society and folk-urban continuum and the participant observation have been two main springboards of the Indian village studies.

However, Dumont's 'caste view' of village and 'civilizational view' of caste is a perspective with difference, though it ignores historicity of Indian society, like the structural-functionalist perspective. The studies of the village community in the 1960s and subsequently have indicated a 'shift' in the theoretical as well as methodological orientations. 'Issue-specific' studies have replaced the earlier holistic studies. Structural analysis has been found more relevant. Methodologically, field-studies combined with survey research, historical data and interdisciplinary input have been conducted. The era of 'holistic' and 'in-depth' studies alone has almost become a matter of history.

Notoo

1. Bernard S. Cohn, 'Notes on the history of the study of Indian society and culture', in Milton Singer and Bernard S. Cohn (eds) *Structure and Change in Indian Society,* Chicago: Aldine Publishing Company, 1968, p. 6.
2. Ibid., p. 7.
3. Ibid., p. 7.
4. Ibid., p. 8.
5. Ibid., p. 8.
6. Ibid., p. 10.
7. Ibid., p. 15.
8. Ibid., p. 23.
9. Louis Dumont, 'The village community from Munro to Maine', *Contributions to Indian Sociology,* No. IX, 1966, p. 67.
10. David G. Mandelbaum, 'Family, Jati, village,' in Milton Singer and Bernard C. Cohn (eds), op. cit., p. 40.
11. Louis Dumont and D.F. Pocock, 'Village studies,' *Contributions to Indian Sociology,* No. I, 1957, pp. 25–32; See also Louis Dumont, 'For a sociology of India: a rejoinder to Dr Bailey,' Contributions to Indian Sociology, No. IV, 1960, pp. 68–89.
12. See, for example, S.C. Dube, *Indian Village,* London: Routledge and Kegan Paul, 1955; M.N. Srinivas (ed.), *India's Villages,* Calcutta: Government of West Bengal Publication, 1955; D.N. Majumdar (ed.), *Rural Profiles,* Lucknow: Ethnographic and Folk-Culture Society, 1955; and McKim Marriott (ed.) *Village India,* Chicago: Chicago University Press, 1955.
13. See, S.C. Dube, *India's Changing Villages,* London: Routledge and Kegan Paul, 1958; T.S. Epstein, *Economic Development and Social Chunge in South India,* Manchester: Manchester University Press, 1962; K. Ishwaran, *Tradition and Economy in Village India,* Bombay: Allied Publishers Pvt. Ltd., 1966, Ramkrishna Mukherjee, *Six Villages of Bengal: A Socio-Economic Survey,* Calcutta: Asiatic Society of Bengal, 1957; and Yogendra Singh, 'The changing power structure of village community: A case study of six villages in Eastern U.P.', in A.R. Desai (ed.), *Rural Sociology in India,* Bombay: Popular Prakashan (4th edition), 1969, pp. 711–723.
14. Ramkrishna Mukherjee, P.C. Joshi, D. Thorner and K. Gough have shown such a methodological orientation in their studies of Indian rural society.

15. See B.R. Chauhan, *A Rajasthan Village,* New Delhi: Associated Publishing House, 1967; and D.N. Majumdar, *Caste and Communication in an Indian Village,* Bombay: Asia Publishing House, 1958.
16. T.K.N. Unnithan, Indra Deva and Yogendra Singh, 'Towards a sociology of culture in India', in T.K.N. Unnithan, Indra Deva and Yogendra Singh (eds) *Towards a Sociology of Culture,* New Delhi: Prentice-Hall of India, 1965.
17. Brij Raj Chauhan, 'Rural studies: a trend report,' in *A Survey of Research in Sociology and Social Anthropology,* Vol. I (ICSSR), Bombay: Popular Prakashan, 1974, p. 48.
18. Ibid., pp. 96–103.
19. M.N. Srinivas, 'Village studies and their significance,'; S.C. Dube, 'The study of Indian village community'; Yogesh Atal, 'Rural studies: Indian village'; and Ramkrishna Mukherjee, 'On village studies in India', in A.R. Desai (ed.), op. cit., 1969, pp. 783–818.
20. M.N. Srinivas, op. cit., 1969, p. 786.
21. Ibid., p. 786.
22. McKim Marriott, op. cit., 1955.
23. See D.P. Mukerji, *Diversities,* Delhi: People's Publishing House, 1958; S.C. Dube, 'The study of complex cultures', in T.K.N. Unnithan, Indra Deva and Yogendra Singh (eds), op. cit., 1965, pp. 404–426; M.N. Srinivas, *Religion and Society among the Coorgs of South India,* Oxford, Oxford University Press, 1952; Yogendra Singh, *Modernization of Indian Tradition,* Delhi: Thompson Press Pvt. Ltd., 1973.
24. M.N. Srinivas, op. cit., 1969, p. 787.
25. See *Contributions to Indian Sociology* (New Series), Vol. 12, No. 1, 1978, for a detailed discussion on Srinivas' *The Remembered Village* (a study of Coorgs).
26. M.N. Srinivas, op. cit., 1969, p. 788.
27. See A.M. Shah, *The Household Dimension of the Family in India,* Delhi: Orient Longman, 1973; Andre Beteille, *Caste, Class and Power,* Bombay: Oxford University Press, 1966; and Anand Chakravarti, Contradictions and Change: Emerging Patterns of Authority in a Rajasthan Village, Delhi: Oxford University Press, 1975.
28. M.N. Srinivas, 'Village studies, participant observation and social science research in India', *Economic and Political Weekly,* Vol, IX, Nos. 22–25 (SN), 1974, p. 1389.
29. Ibid., p. 1389.
30. Ibid., p. 1389.

31. Ibid., p. 1389.
32. T.S. Epstein, op. cit., 1962; and F.G. Bailey, *Caste and the Economic Frontier,* Manchester: Manchester University Press, 1957.
33. Satish Saberwal, *Mobile Men: Limits to Social Change in Urban Punjab,* New Delhi: Vikas Publishing House, 1976; and Owen M. Lynch, 'The politics of untouchability: a case from Agra, India', in M. Singer and B.S. Cohn (ed.), op. cit., 1968, pp. 209–313.
34. Biplab Dasgupta, 'A typology of village socio-economic systems from Indian village studies,' *Economic and Political Weekly,* Vol. X, Nos. 33–35 (SN), 1975, p. 1395.
35. Ibid., p. 1397.
36. S.C. Dube, in A.R. Desai (ed.), op. cit. 1969.
37. Ibid., pp. 790–791.
38. Ibid., p. 792.
39. Ibid., p. 792.
40. Ibid., p. 792.
41. Ibid., p. 793.
42. Ibid., p. 793.
43. Yogesh Atal, in A.R. Desai (ed.), op. cit., 1969, p, 801.
44. Ibid., pp. 803–804.
45. A.R. Desai, 'Village studies in India: Introduction', in A.R. Desai (ed.), op. cit., 1969, p. 784.
46. Ramkrishna Mukherjee, in A.R. Desai (ed.), op. cit., 1969.
47. Ramkrishna Mukherjee, *Dynamics of a Rural Society,* Berlin: Akademie Verlag, 1957.
48. McKim Marriott (ed.), *Village India,* op. cit., 1955.
49. M.N. Srinivas (ed.), *India's Villages,* op. cit., 1955.
50. L. Dumont and D.F. Pocock, 'Village studies', op. cit., 1957.
51. Robert Redfield and Milton Singer, 'Foreword', in McKim Marriott (ed.), *Village India,* op. cit., 1955, p. vii.
52. David G. Mandelbaum, 'The world view of the Kota', in McKim Marriott (ed.), op. cit., pp. 223–254.
53. Robert Redfield and Milton Singer, op. cit., 1955, p. ix.
54. Ibid., p. ix.
55. Ibid., p. x.
56. Kathleen Gough, 'The social structure of a Tanjore village', in McKim Marriott (ed.), op. cit., 1955, p. 41.

57. M.N. Srinivas, 'The social system of a Mysore village', in McKim Marriott (ed.), op. cit., 1955, p. 1.
58. Kathleen E. Gough, op. cit., in McKim Marriott (ed.), op. cit., 1955.
59. Ibid., p. 51.
60. Bernard S. Cohn, 'The changing status of a depressed caste', in McKim Marriott (ed.), *Village India,* op. cit., 1955, pp. 53–77.
61. Alan R. Beals, 'Interplay among the factors of change in a Mysore village', in McKim Marriott (ed.), *Village India,* op. cit., 1955, p. 80.
62. Gitel P. Steed, 'Notes on an approach to a study of personality formation in a Hindu village in Gujarat', in McKim Marriott (ed.), *Village India,* op. cit., 1955, p. 107.
63. Ibid., p. 107.
64. Ibid., pp. 107–117.
65. Oscar Lewis, 'Peasant culture in India and Mexico: a comparative analysis', in McKim Marriott (ed.), *Village India,* op. cit., 1955, p. 145.
66. Ibid., p. 146.
67. Ibid., pp. 146–147.
68. Ibid., p. 147.
69. Oscar Lewis, *Life in a Mexican Village: Tepoztlan Restudied,* Urbana, University of Illinois Press, 1951, p. xx.
70. Ibid., p. xxi.
71. Oscar Lewis, in McKim Marriott (ed.), op. cit., 1955, p. 160.
72. Ibid., p. 161.
73. Ibid., p. 161.
74. Ibid., p. 162.
75. Ibid., p. 162.
76. Ibid., p. 162.
77. Ibid., p. 168.
78. Ibid., p. 169.
79. McKim Marriott, 'Little communities in an indigenous civilization', in McKim Marriott (ed.) *Village India,* op. cit., 1955, p. 171.
80. Ibid., p. 173.
81. Ibid., p. 175.
82. Ibid., p. 176.
83. Ibid., p. 172.
84. Ibid., pp. 178–179.

85. Ibid., pp. 179–180.
86. M.N. Srinivas (ed.), *India's Villages,* op. cit., 1955.
87. Ibid., 'Introduction', pp. 1–14.
88. Louis Dumont and D.F. Pocock, op. cit., 1957, p. 23.
89. Ibid., p. 23.
90. Ibid., pp. 23–24.
91. Ibid., p. 24.
92. Ibid., p. 24.
93. Ibid., p. 25.
94. Ibid., p. 25.
95. Ibid., p. 25.
96. Ibid., p. 25.
97. Ibid., p. 26.
98. Ibid., p. 41.
99. Ibid., p. 41.
100. Louis Dumont, 'The village community from Munro to Maine', *Contributions to Indian Sociology,* No. IX, 1966, p. 67.
101. See Louis Dumont's two essays: (1) 'The conception of kingship in ancient India', and (2) 'Fundamental problem in the sociology of caste', in his *Religion, Politics and History of India,* Paris: Mouton Publishers, 1970.
102. Sir Henry Sumner Maine, *Village Communities in the East and West,* London: J. Murray, 1871.
103. S.C. Dube, *Indian Village,* op. cit., 1955.
104. Ibid., pp. 2–3.
105. Ibid., p. 304.
106. Ibid., p. 6.
107. Ibid., p. 222.
108. D.N. Majumdar, op. cit., 1958.
109. Oscor Lewis, *Village Life in Northern India,* Urbana: University of Illinois, 1958.
110. See F.G. Bailey, 1957; T.S. Epstein, 1962; Andre Beteille, 1966; Kathleen E. Gough, 1955; K. Ishwaran, 1967; Ramkrishna Mukherjee, 1957; M.S.A. Rao, *Urbanization and Social Change,* New Delhi: Orient Longmans, 1967, and K.L. Sharma, *The Changing Rural Stratification System,* Orient Longman, New Delhi, 1974.

111. K. Ishwaran, *Change and Continuity in India's Villages,* New York: Columbia University Press, 1970.
112. K. Ishwaran, 'Introduction', in K. Ishwaran (ed.), op. cit., 1970, p. 1.
113. Ibid., p. 2.
114. Yogendra Singh, 'Chanukhera: cultural change in Eastern Uttar Pradesh', in K. Ishwaran (ed.), op. cit., 1970, pp. 269–270.
115. See Articles in K. Ishwaran (ed.), op. cit., 1970.
116. Kathleen E. Gough, 'Palakkara: social and religious change in Central Kerala', in K. Ishwaran (ed.), op. cit., 1970, p. 156.
117. Joan P. Mencher, 'A Tamil village: changing socio-economic structure in Madras State', in K. Ishwaran (ed.), op. cit., 1970, pp. 197–218.
118. K. Ishwaran, 'Introducticn', op. cit., 1970, p. 14.
119. Goran Djurfeldt and Staffan Lindberg, *Pills Against Poverty,* New Delhi: Oxford and IBH Publishing Co., 1976.
120. Ibid., pp. 15–17.
121. Ibid., p. 18.
122. Ibid., p. 24.
123. Ibid., p. 26.
124. Biplab Dasgupta, *Village Studies in the Third World* (ed.), Delhi: Hindustan Publishing Corporation, 1978.
125. Biplab Dasgupta, 'Introduction', in Biplab Dasgupta (ed.), op. cit., 1978, pp. 3–4.
126. Ibid., pp. 6–7.
127. G. Parthasarathy, 'Indian village studies and the village poor', in Biplab Dasgupta (ed.), op. cit., 1978, pp. 149–164.
128. Ibid., pp. 160–61.
129. Cf. G. Parthasarathy, op. cit., 1978, p. 155.
130. G. Parthasarathy, op. cit., 1978, p. 163.

Chapter 6

Conclusion

Can anyone conclude decisively about the nature of sociology in India? It seems to us that a given piece of writing (research monograph or an analytical paper) could certainly be evaluated in terms of its theoretical assumptions, research strategies and data, but discerning of dominance of one or other theoretic and methodological orientation at a given point of time in the history of sociology in India becomes really a difficult task. Moreover, the exercise carried out by us remains mainly interpretational. It is neither historical nor empirical as we have already stated in the introduction. Our effort has been geared to the analysis of those studies whose theoretic and methodological orientations have not been quite clear to us and perhaps to others as well, but which have had serious implications for sociology as a discipline and for understanding of Indian society. We have also discussed some of the studies whose theoretic and methodological orientations seem to be quite demystified, but their implications are again of far-reaching nature for ideologizing Indian sociology. Alternative to these orientations has been suggested in the indigenization of theory and method of study. But this too is not free from limitations. Indigenization, if implemented, might result into a variety of parochial, regional and zonal sociologies in the name of scientific inquiries.

Indian sociology is crossbred by the positivist and the idealist traditions. The positivistic input has come from both American and

British sociology and social anthropology. The impact of idealist tradition has come mainly from Max Weber's contributions. However, several studies of class relations, agrarian structure and movements have also been conducted from the Marxian perspective. Some studies of family and marriage have been guided by the structuralist perspective. The question is about the nature of input of these approaches and perspectives in sociological studies of Indian society.

We have tried to understand theory, method and data as parts of the sociology of knowledge perspective in Indian sociology in general and in the studies of social stratification and village community in particular. Talcott Parson's structural functionalism, R.K. Merton's functional analysis, Radcliffe-Brown's functionalism, structuralism of Levi-Strauss, historical dialectical materialism of Karl Marx, and Max Weber's Verstehen or ideal-type constructions have influenced sociological studies in India. We have examined these studies by keeping in view the above theoretical constructs.

The emphasis on universal concepts and categories for studying Indian society has been laid mainly due to two assumptions: (a) Western frameworks, concepts and classifications are assumed as scientific; and (b) Science is viewed as universal. Hence, acceptance of the Western theoretic formulations and research strategies. Radhakamal Mukerjee advocated a universalistic sociology as he believed in generality of meta-scientific assumptions. D.P. Mukerji accepted Marxism as a science but with significant modifications at the level of its application for the study of Indian society. Cultural and national identity was considered as a significant factor by D.P. Mukerji. However, universality of science was considered by A.K. Saran as a Western concept, hence unacceptable due to its particularistic aud culture-specific origin. G.S. Ghurye was initially influenced by the early diffusionist approach of British social anthropology, but subsequently he switched to the studies of Indian society from Indological and anthropological perspectives. Perhaps, I.P. Desai is one sociologist who has conducted studies without borrowing concepts and categories from the Western sociology.

The governmental policies and programmes have certainly influenced some sociologists, hence studies of Community

Development Programmes, family planning, Panchayati Raj, Antyodaya, twenty-points programme, etc.

The thrust of the debate on the nature of Indian sociology can be seen as follows: (a) Sociology as a reflection of general and universal scientific concepts and categories, (b) as a unique culture-specific discipline and (c) as a 'mix' of the two. The last refers to the view that the general principles when applied to specific situation might get modified, and the unique situations might be found relevant for understanding other forms of social situations. However, generality and universality of science is claimed by sociologists of the non-Marxist as well as by those who have Marxist dispositions.

The debate on sociology in India pointedly starts in 1957 with the beginning of publication of the journal *Contributions to Indian Sociology*, by Louis Dumont and D.F. Pocock. There is no clear order or sequence in the debate regarding raising of points. Theory and method have been debated more than the field of study. Between theory and method, theory has received more attention than method. However, the two are not exclusive points in any discipline, including sociology. Yogendra Singh has contributed perhaps more than any other Indian sociologist by providing classifications and categories of the studies of social stratification, social change, social structure and culture. In fact, he has periodized and classified sociological studies on India covering twenty-five years – from 1952 to 1977. Singh has shown more concern for theoretic orientations than methodologies and data collection in systematization of descriptive and narrative accounts. However, Singh prefers a combination of general and specific aspects of sociology for evolving a suitable framework for studying Indian society.

Dumont's preference for descriptive sociology for India in view of India's oneness does not find a favour from Singh. Dumont's sociology is treated more as a value-loaded sociology than a sociology of values. F.G. Bailey too considers it narrow, static and out of context. Dumont's ideas of oneness, unity in diversity, hierarchy, pollution-purity, and social organization are unacceptable, due to the fact that they have been relegated to the background by the force of factors of social change. Study of 'structural facts' finds more favour from sociologists today than the study of 'cultural facts'.

All the contributors to the debate claim 'positivism' in their analyses. Dumont, in response to the criticism of his view on Indian sociology, reformulates his position by pleading a case for a combination of the external view with the internal view, and pleads that his position may be treated as positive-cum-subjective. However, A.K. Saran considers such a combination as positivistic hybris. Saran's view is that positivism in the present form is a provincial standpoint. Saran observes that ontologically, man is a non-being abstraction, and therefore, comparison of one culture with another is simply meaningless. Dumont calls it Saran's cultural 'solipsism'. Whatever may be the apparent differences regarding the views of Dumont, Saran and Saxena accord priority to the peculiarity of Indian society in one way or other. Scholars of this variety have not taken economic formation and its ramifications as relevant phenomena for sociological investigation.

The question is of relevant approach for studying Indian society. False cosmopolitanism and false humanitarianism must go as suggested by Uberoi. Notions of positivism have created falsehood of universal application of scientific method and concepts of westernization, etc. and have created again a feeling of false humanitarianism. The reality perhaps is that caste solidarities have been revived and restrengthened as a result of several such studies. Singh rightly refers to sociology as a system of operational concepts of societal self-consciousness. It would be proper to see how far colonial/traditional approaches, concepts and methods of study have continued, and how far they have been substituted by new approaches, concepts and methods.

Sociology in India is processual in nature. In the 1950s, Western approaches and methods were accepted. In the 1960s, they were seriously reviewed. In the late 1960s, new theoretical directions and fields of study were explored; and in the 1970s, these were given due credibility. But specific theoretic orientations have co-existed and this has facilitated theoretical cross-comparisons with substantiation of facts. Y. Singh gives more emphasis on systematization and classifications with a 'positivistic' bias than on ontologically-determined concepts and categories. Ramkrishna Mukherjee pleads for a new framework which he names as 'inductive-inferential' orientation. It is more of a logico-deductive exercise and straitjacketed.

Finally, we have dealt with the question whether sociology in India could be nationalistic or it could be only a part of general sociology. The question is: Is there a general or universal sociology? Sociology in India has been alleged to be Hindu Sociology. Modernity is said to be a 'provincial' concept. What is objectivity? Because of the above apprehensions, it could simply be the subjectivity of a dominant society.

In the 1950s, studies on social stratification and village community were influenced by academic moorings of the British and American sociologists and anthropologists. Participant observation was promoted by the scholars having impact of the British social anthropology; and tools such as interview, schedule and questionnaire were popularized by the scholars, influenced by American sociologists and anthropologists. By accepting these research devices, superiority of the western approaches and concepts were admitted. Functionalist orientation was basic to American as well as British scholars. Concepts of caste, class and power were operationalized from Weberian point of view. However, the culture-specificity and historicity, which Weber made as the basis of his concepts and classifications have not been examined seriously while accepting his frame of analysis for studying Indian society. This is true not only in regard to the application of Weberian concepts, it is equally true about the application of Marxian, psychological, and Warner's approaches for studying social stratification and village community. Indigenization of approaches, concepts and methods of study has been suggested as a remedy for the alien approaches, because they are rooted in the experiences of other societies, particularly the industrially advanced countries.

We have discussed the problem of the use of participant observation vs aggregate data analysis, village as a unit of study, relevance of comparative approach, and culturology vs structural analysis. The shift is toward issue-specific studies with an emphasis on understanding of structural facts. A combination of intensive field-work, survey research, historical data and interdisciplinary input is preferred than participant observation or schedule alone as the method of study. Today, 'relevance' of approach and method of study has become the main concern in Indian sociology.

Index